Raising the Achievement of All Pupils within an Inclusive Setting

Schools everywhere are concerned with raising standards according to government requirements, particularly for those pupils who could be termed 'more able'. The key challenges revolve around government initiatives such as 'Every Child Matters', independent learning, inclusion and differentiation, thus making learning effective and successful for all pupils.

The authors of this highly engaging book carried out extensive analysis of twelve key schools, selected for their representation of common challenging educational circumstances including working with children from:

- multilingual and multi-ethnic communities
- low socio-economic and disadvantaged communities
- small rural schools and big inner-city communities
- schools with high levels of special educational needs.

All the case-study schools subscribe to the educational ethos of creating an environment for all pupils to *discover* their gifts and talents, and the authors show clearly how these findings can be applied in any school.

Raising the Achievement of All Pupils within an Inclusive Setting describes the strategies that have been developed to provide equal opportunities for all pupils, whilst accommodating different individual needs and rates of development. A major focus is on identifying and resolving underachievement in schools.

Drawing upon intensive interviews with staff, pupils, parents and governors, the authors provide practical guidance for successfully raising motivation, achievement and educational standards in any school environment.

Teachers, Gifted and Talented coordinators and school leaders seeking guidance and inspiration from real-life schools will benefit from the down-to-earth, achievable advice offered in this book.

Belle Wallace works as a consultant on the Education of Gifted and Talented Pupils, both nationally and internationally. She is also Director of TASC International and immediate past president of NACE.

Raising the Achievement of All Pupils within an Inclusive Setting

Practical strategies for developing best practice

Belle Wallace,
Sue Leyden,
Diane Montgomery,
Carrie Winstanley,
Michael Pomerantz
and Sally Fitton

Routledge
Taylor & Francis Group

LONDON AND NEW YORK

First published 2010
by Routledge
2 Park Square, Milton Park, Abingdon, Oxon OX14 4RN

Simultaneously published in the USA and Canada
by Routledge
270 Madison Avenue, New York, NY 10016

Routledge is an imprint of the Taylor & Francis Group, an informa business

© 2010 Belle Wallace, Sue Leyden, Diane Montgomery,
Carrie Winstanley, Michael Pomerantz and Sally Fitton

Typeset in Sabon by
Keystroke, Tettenhall, Wolverhampton
Printed and bound in Great Britain by
TJ International Ltd, Padstow, Cornwall

Every effort has been made to contact copyright holders for their
permission to reprint material in this book. The publishers would be
grateful to hear from any copyright holder who is not here
acknowledged, and will undertake to rectify any errors or omissions in
future editions of this book.

British Library Cataloguing in Publication Data
A catalogue record for this book is available from the British Library

Library of Congress Cataloging-in-Publication Data
Raising the achievement of all pupils within an inclusive setting : practical
strategies for developing best practice / Belle Wallace . . . [et al.].
    p. cm.
  1. Inclusive education—Great Britain. I. Wallace, Belle.
  LC1203.G7R35 2010
  371.9'0460941—dc22   2009022247

ISBN 10: 0–415–54948–5 (hbk)
ISBN 10: 0–415–54949–3 (pbk)
ISBN 10: 0–203–86488–3 (ebk)

ISBN 13: 978–0–415–54948–6 (hbk)
ISBN 13: 978–0–415–54949–3(pbk)
ISBN 13: 978–0–203–86488–3 (ebk)

Dedication

It has been a joyous life experience to work with dedicated teachers who see their role as facilitators of learning: they are always passionate about developing learners' capacities to learn; they see their educational function as that of enabling others to discover, to create, to question, to explore, to make decisions and judgements, to see and to solve problems. These life mentors and vocational facilitators are concerned that the learners in their care fulfil their intellectual potential and become socially and emotionally responsible for themselves and others.

It has been equally joyous to see learners grow and flourish in the classrooms of these outstanding educators: learners are fully aware of the power and influence of those teachers who make them feel special, worthwhile, enthusiastic, committed. Learners do know when teachers really care about them: they do know which lessons are interesting, motivating, exhilarating.

Hence this text is dedicated to the many teachers who can be called facilitators and mentors in the true sense that their professional joy and satisfaction comes from seeing children and young people thrive and flourish in their classrooms.

Contents

Illustrations

Tables

Contributors

Sally Fitton is a Secondary School Improvement Adviser for Derbyshire local authority working in partnership with a range of schools in raising achievement. Her additional responsibility is for developing provision for gifted and talented pupils across Derbyshire, with a particular emphasis on encouraging teachers to reflect on their practice and develop strategies that address underachievement of gifted and talented pupils.

Sue Leyden is an independent educational consultant and a chartered educational psychologist. During her many years as an LEA advisor/inspector for SEN, she was a lead member of a team developing the curriculum for very able pupils and researching their academic and personal needs. She is the author of *Supporting the Child of Exceptional Ability at Home and School*, now in its third edition.

Diane Montgomery, PhD, is Emeritus Professor in Education at Middlesex University, London. She is a qualified teacher and chartered psychologist specialising in research on giftedness and learning difficulties. She has authored and run distance-learning programmes in MA Gifted Education, MA SEN, and MA SEBD and MA SpLD (Dyslexia). She writes extensively on gifted education, able underachievers, double exceptionality, dyslexia, spelling, behaviour problems, appraisal and learning difficulties.

Michael Pomerantz, PhD, retired at Easter 2009. He was an Associate Tutor to the DEdCPsy Course in initial training for Educational Psychologists at the University of Sheffield. He was also a Senior Educational Psychologist and team manager in Derbyshire providing services to a range of primary, secondary and special schools. In retirement Michael is active with writing and is a psychological consultant to a major three-year, ESRC funded project based at the Universities of Glasgow and Stirling helping to develop research communities.

Belle Wallace is immediate past President of the National Association for Able Children in Education (NACE); Editor of *Gifted Education International* (UK: AB Academic Publishers); and an international consultant on provision for gifted and talented children. Belle has been a member of the Executive Committee for the World Council for Gifted and Talented Children (WCGTC) and has published extensively on the development of problem-solving curricula across the multiple capacities for all levels of students. She is currently Director of TASC International.

Carrie Winstanley, PhD, currently works with undergraduate and post-graduate education students, specifically concerning inclusion and able children with specific learning needs. She runs workshops and activities for children in museums and galleries and researches into pedagogy and the ethics of provision for the able considering practical ideas with a strong theoretical grounding.

Introduction

In the first chapter, Belle Wallace examines the differences between the concepts of achievement and attainment and then discusses the possible causes of underachievement. She suggests a Typology of Underachievement that, although slanted towards more able pupils, applies equally to all pupils when the school seeks to discover and celebrate all pupils' gifts across the wide spectrum of multiple capacities. The chapter also highlights some of the successful strategies used by the schools in the original case-study research. (See *Raising the Achievement of Able, Gifted and Talented Pupils within an Inclusive School Framework*. Copies of this summary can be obtained from publications@nace.co.uk.)

In Chapter 2, Sue Leyden discusses the importance of the development of positive self-concept and maintains that the social and emotional needs of children and young people should be at the very heart of educational thinking. She strongly argues that children who are unhappy or unsettled do not flourish in school and are unlikely to make best use of their learning experiences, and most probably will underachieve. The chapter examines the key factors that underpin successful social, emotional and personal development, with a special reference to potential high flyers. Sue threads the chapter with case studies that illustrate the causes of underachievement of some able learners.

Diane Montgomery concentrates on exploring the syndrome of dual or double exceptionality (2E) in Chapter 3, the term which is used to describe those learners who are potentially very able or who have a special gift in a performance or skill area, but who also have a special educational need (SEN) such as dyslexia, or ADHD. Her major theme is that in many potentially able learners with special educational needs, the potential 'gift' is 'masked'. Diane outlines strategies that help teachers to recognise and alleviate underachievement of these learners.

Chapter 4 examines the concept of challenge that is clearly vital in supporting all children and keeping them motivated in school. Carrie Winstanley considers the question of the nature of challenge and how teachers can ensure that learners are engaged in activities they find personally satisfying. The chapter also looks at some of the key aspects of best practice: cognitive challenge through appropriate questioning; thinking skills and philosophy (Philosophy for Children); and independent and personalised problem-solving (TASC – Thinking Actively in a Social Context).

In Chapter 5, Michael Pomerantz examines the potential of Pupil Research Communities to accommodate learners' strong need to express themselves far more creatively than applies at present in many schools. He argues that many pupils could offer so much more to their schools if they were given real-life, problem-solving opportunities. Pupils could promote social justice, reduce marginalisation, encourage participatory citizenship and reduce waste of time and effort. He suggests ways that schools could effectively utilise the energy of pupils that is often diverted into antisocial behaviour.

Chapter 6 investigates the key features that underpin successful leadership and curriculum provision that constitute the significant drivers in tackling the underachievement of all pupils, including the more able. Sally Fitton discusses the range of common principles that were found within the case-study schools and these principles are expanded in more detail here. The vision of the case-study schools is not one that clings to a narrow elitist view of recognising a small percentage of pupils as gifted and talented, but is one that is concerned to raise the achievement of all pupils within an inclusive context. The practitioners in these schools continually strive to provide more effective learning pathways for all, and in doing so, outstanding provision for gifted learners is being developed.

Chapter 1

Tackling underachievement

Maximising opportunities for all pupils in an inclusive setting

Belle Wallace

We are sentient, dynamic beings capable of change: but we can be trapped not only in the learned sense of what we are not, but also in a powerful negative mirror image of ourselves that we perceive emanating from others. Yet, we can be released through enabling interactions with those special mentors who offer constant and strong scaffolding that we are, indeed, of great worth and significance as individuals with potential.

(Belle Wallace, 2008a)

Introduction

During the years 2006–2007, the writers who have contributed to this book carried out case-study researches in twelve schools: five secondary and seven primary schools in the UK. The overall purpose of the case studies was to highlight the practical strategies that successfully enabled the transformation of pupils' *high potential* into *high achievement*. The initial research was jointly funded by London Gifted and Talented (London G + T) and the National Association for Able Children in Education (NACE). A summary of this research is published by NACE (Wallace *et al.* 2007) (in conjunction with London G + T) entitled *Raising the Achievement of Able, Gifted and Talented Pupils within an Inclusive School Framework*. (Copies of the summary can be obtained from publications@nace.co.uk.)

The aim of this book is to explore teaching and learning strategies that will maximise opportunities for *all* learners' gifts and talents to be discovered and nurtured; hence, we have some reservations in referring to some pupils as 'gifted', especially with regard to very young learners. Therefore, throughout the text, we use a variety of terms such as 'able', 'more able', potentially able', as well as 'gifted' and 'potentially gifted'. It is only life experiences and appropriate opportunities, together with the determination and stamina of each individual, that will bring potential gifts and talents to fruition. In addition, throughout this text, the schools that are referred to are the twelve case-study schools that took part in the original case-study research; however, the authors make generalisations about best practice that apply to all schools.

This chapter summarises a range of attitudes and strategies that underpin successful schools: undoubtedly, high-level leadership and appropriate curriculum provision are significant drivers in tackling the underachievement of our able pupils. The vision of the schools in the original case study is not one that clings to a narrow elitist view of recognising a small percentage of pupils as gifted and talented, but one that is concerned to raise the achievement of *all* pupils within an inclusive context. In her chapter, Sally Leyden describes how the leaders in these case-study schools have created a safe environment within an ethos and climate of high aspirations, expectations and respect.

The schools that participated in the original case-study research all believed and practised a policy of inclusion – providing rich and varied opportunities for *all* pupils to discover their gifts and talents through opportunities to engage in enriched and extended provision. All the schools in the research were concerned to provide curricular opportunities that would challenge the potentially very able while also supporting and extending learners at all stages of development. The schools that participated in the original research were all urban schools with a wide range of catchment areas and, consequently, a very wide and demanding range of challenges that needed to be surmounted.

All the schools in the study were concerned to develop whole-school awareness of possible causes of underachievement, and also to take appropriate action to prevent the syndrome of underachievement occurring. The researchers spent considerable time in each school accessing relevant qualitative and quantitative data: school records and logbooks, Standard Attainment Test (SAT) results, Ofsted reports, examination results, National Quality Standards achievements, NACE Challenge Award achievements and evidence of other various performance and achievement awards. Researchers also observed lessons and interviewed members of the senior management, members of staff including Gifted and Talented (G + T) coordinators, a selection of pupils, parents/carers and governors. This qualitative information was richly informative, reflecting the dynamic, living research evidence that should lie at the centre of detailed case-study research.

Although the purpose of the original research was to analyse the components that constitute excellent provision for G + T pupils, it was soon obvious that since all schools had developed a policy of inclusion, what was considered best practice for G + T pupils applied to *all* pupils. Hence this text, although slanted towards the needs of pupils with high potential, is also focused on the needs of all learners.

See Appendix 1 on page 191 for a brief summary of the case-study school contexts.

As the lead researcher of the original case studies, I was privileged to work with a renowned team of education experts who all have long and distinguished careers forged through living experience of dealing with educational issues at the practical grass roots of classrooms. They are well known nationally (and also internationally) for their personal commitment to the well-being and development of learners, teachers and parents; they are equally well known for their passion for advocating the provision of engaging and inspiring educational opportunities for all learners in an inclusive setting. Consequently, they have all spent their professional lives being concerned to analyse the intrinsic meaning of 'achievement', together with the causes of 'underachievement', and to bring about effective educational practice to circumvent the widespread syndrome of 'underachievement' that has, unfortunately, become a major challenge in many of our schools throughout the UK.

After the completion of the original action research study (2007), all the writers felt that, as a team, we needed to extend the summary report by adding our own reflective thoughts based on our collective lifetime of promoting what we would call 'an enabling, enriching, extending curriculum'. The text is not intended to be a criticism of schools: its purpose is to provide a base for reflective practitioners to debate and celebrate those educational practices which are successfully motivating learners and to consider how they can extend their best practice. We hope that the text will become a standard reference book and a sounding board for initial and continuing professional development (CPD), and that teams of teachers will engage in discussion and debate with their pupils and pupils' parents/carers using the text as a stimulus for further thinking and problem-solving around school-based issues. Throughout the text, readers are invited to reflect upon and to discuss the many issues that challenge all teachers in today's classrooms.

What do we mean by 'achievement' and 'underachievement'?

The following section discusses the meaning of 'achievement' and 'under-achievement', as the terms are used throughout this text, and can be used as the basis for staff discussion so that working definitions can be adopted with common understanding across the school. The section also suggests a classification framework for 'Typologies of Underachievement': this can be used to heighten teacher awareness and, possibly, to extend existing conceptions.

In a text that aims to discuss effective strategies to promote achievement, it is essential that we also discuss what we mean by underachievement. Both terms are relative to the individual and also to the aims of the particular education system and its values: both terms need to be viewed from the basis of 'What do teachers, learners and parents/carers regard as "achievement" and its negative image "underachievement"?'

It is important to emphasise at the beginning that although there are a number of inter-related general factors which bring about the overall syndrome of underachievement, essentially each individual has a unique set of characteristics. Hence, although we can discuss underachievement in *general* terms, the assessment of the causes of underachievement and the possible intervention (remediation) strategies need to focus on the *individual* learner and his or her special characteristics and needs. Also, we must recognise that there are some causes of underachievement that are beyond the power and capacity of a single school to remove: personal, home and community factors can be completely debilitating. Nevertheless, schools and teachers can and do make a difference. When schools promote personalised learning and involve learners in the negotiation of *what* is learned and *how* it is learned, then learners have ownership and a sense of being a partner in the learning process.

Throughout the text, we will use the term word *achievement* to mean the outcome of effort, learning, perseverance, self-belief and encouragement. It involves the individual experiencing challenge, making discoveries and reaping the rewards, either intrinsic or extrinsic, of effort and application. An ethos of achievement can be defined as one in which there are high expectations and high standards set in *all* spheres of activity, where effort is supported and where *all* learners are encouraged to 'aim high', to learn from mistakes and to go on to experience and enjoy success. Consequently we use the term *underachievement* to signify lack of the above.

In contrast, we will use the term *attainment* to refer to pupils' attaining in terms of measured levels obtained in SATs in literacy and numeracy and the General Certificate of Education (GCSE) levels A to C.

As stated above, the major theme running through the text is how we can promote a school policy of inclusion where *all* learners' needs are met. However, within this overall ethos of inclusion, we will, nevertheless, discuss strategies that can be developed to cater for the particular needs of potentially able learners.

While classifying the behaviour patterns of underachieving but potentially able pupils, it is essential to note the positive characteristics of able underachievers when they are motivated. We could term these characteristics 'switch on lights'.

Box 1.1   Able underachievers: switch on lights!

When motivated, able underachievers:

- are inventive and original – often thinking 'outside the box';
- are quick to learn new concepts and to pose problems, and quick to suggest ingenious solutions – especially those unrelated to academic school tasks;

- ask provocative questions with regard to life issues and people;
- persevere, particularly when the relationship with the teacher is positive and personally supportive;
- are surprisingly wise about everyday problems and common-sense issues;
- are streetwise and aware of how the 'real' world works;
- are perceptive in discussions about people's motives, needs and frailties, especially about their teachers;
- are responsive in a secure environment;
- enjoy the overview and bigger picture of a task or activity.

How do we assess underachievement with regard to potentially able learners? In any discussion concerning the assessment of the under-achievement of potentially able learners, we need to consider a number of dimensions. Box 1.2 gives a range of possible strategies that schools may use.

Box 1.2 Strategies for assessing possible underachievement

- Significant discrepancy between verbal and non-verbal scores on an individual or group test of intelligence – high non-verbal score as against low verbal score.
- Professional teacher assessment of pupils' strengths across the full range of multiple capacities (intelligences). This can be the result of teacher observation or linked with an inventory of char-acteristics typifying behaviours across the full range of multiple capacities (intelligences).
- An indication of underachievement as measured against school norms such as SATs, class tests, examinations.
- Teachers' judgement of personal underachievement perceived with regard to pupils' self-confidence, self-esteem, motivation and social maturity.
- Good achievement in one area of the curriculum, but not in others.
- The intuitive perception of teachers, particularly in any form of creative activity.
- Analysis of the personal theories which pupils hold about concepts such as 'intelligence', 'ability' and 'potential.
- Peer-group nomination.
- Personal testimony of pupils and self-nomination.

- Case-study reports from parents/carers/guardians.
- Diagnostic assessment of learning difficulties, and disabilities or sensory impairments.
- Professional assessment of underachievement estimated against perceived potential revealed on group or individual tests of 'intelligence'. These tests can be individually administered by an educational psychologist, or may be a group test such as the Cognitive Ability Test (CAT).

How can we begin to classify the typologies of underachievers?

We can also think of underachievers as falling into a broad range of behaviour typologies. Any pupil will possibly demonstrate a range of characteristics that may be associated with any one typology, or may overlap with several typologies.

However, used flexibly, the typologies can highlight certain characteristics and sensitise teacher *and pupil* awareness. Box 1.3 outlines a range of typologies related to underachievement. Teachers can use this box as a basis for discussion and possible diagnosis of certain kinds of behaviour that may be associated with underachievement.

Box 1.3 Typologies of underachievers

Conforming coasters

Learners falling into this typology could be termed 'invisible underachievers'.

Observable indicators – learners could show some of the following; they may:

- quietly meet teachers' expectations by doing what is required;
- remember and repeat the content of lessons in tests;
- never volunteer questions or answers but can supply both when asked directly;
- be well-behaved and get on with tasks without asking for help;
- complete the number of required pages neatly;
- decorate finished work;
- seldom make an error;

- seldom make a contribution to discussion;
- be consulted by other learners;
- quickly catch up on missed work.

Impatient inattentives

Learners falling into this typology could be termed 'butterfly learners'.
   Observable indicators – learners could show some of the following;
they may:

- appear not to be listening but always know the answers when asked;
- find difficulty in sitting still and listening but always know what to do;
- interfere with others' group work;
- prefer active learning when they are engaged in doing something;
- make leaps in stages of learning, often seeing the end result without working things through;
- be impatient with the detail or routine;
- be reluctant to write things down;
- apparently lack sustained concentration;
- be easily distracted;
- be at the root of jokes and good-humoured mischief;
- complete homework scrappily but correctly;
- prefer socialising with peers.

Apathetic non-engagers

These learners seem disinterested in most, if not all, school activities
and could be termed 'mental absentees'.
   Observable indicators – learners could show some of the following;
they may:

- appear 'bored' in all lessons;
- watch the clock all the time;
- be uninterested in school achievement;
- be absorbed in a private world;
- seldom complete work;
- be withdrawn and solitary;
- be lethargic and lacking energy;
- be irregular attendees.

Risk avoiders

These learners seem unable to take risks and play safe within any situation. They could be termed 'safe players'.

Observable indicators – learners could show some of the following; they may:

- appear to have a low sense of self-efficacy;
- avoid a challenge when it is presented;
- opt out of new experiences;
- rely on others for decisions;
- be shy and lacking in self-confidence;
- have high *apparent* self-confidence;
- have internalised a belief that ability is largely fixed, and cannot be developed;
- resist working hard at tasks they find difficult;
- be reticent to volunteer;
- be unable to play a leadership role;
- express personal inadequacy.

Disaffected disengaged

These learners are challenging and disruptive and could be termed the 'actively anti' or 'hard to reach'.

Observable indicators – learners could show some of the following; they may:

- be vocally anti-school and critical of its values;
- be abrasively, unkindly and perceptively humorous;
- be impatient and intolerant of others;
- be creative leaders of malcontents;
- be prone to extreme moodiness and bad temper;
- be apparently self-sufficient and indifferent to school standards;
- seldom complete work;
- be irregular attendees;
- be defensive and astute in self-defence;
- be well-endowed with low cunning and survival skills;
- manipulate others;
- be at risk of being excluded.

Doubly or multiply exceptional

These learners have:

- specific learning disabilities (SpLD) such as dyslexia, dyspraxia, attention deficit/hyperactvity disorder (ADHD);
- physical, sensory and/or medical difficulties (PSM);
- social, emotional and behavioural difficulties (SEBD);
- communication and interaction difficulties: autistic spectrum disorders (ASD), particularly Asperger's syndrome (AS); Down's syndrome (DS); speech, language and communication needs (SLCN).

These learners may be identified as having a disability and their giftedness can be ignored. They could be termed 'masked gifted'. (See Chapter 3 on double exceptionality.)

Observable indicators – there is an enormous range of observable indicators that collectively encompass these syndromes, conditions and behaviours. However, learners may show the following common characteristics:

- a gap between oral and written work;
- problems in relationships with peer group;
- avoidance of trying new activities;
- dislike of group work;
- failure to complete school work;
- dissatisfaction with their achievements;
- lack of concentration;
- poor attitudes to school;
- dislike of drill and rote learning (those with AS/ASD may enjoy the safety of this);
- have a low self-image;
- set unrealistic goals.

What are some of the possible causes of underachievement?

The following issues can be used as the basis for discussion and schools can crystallise the challenges they are seeking to overcome with regard to their own school population.

There is never a single cause of underachievement: the causes derive from a complex interplay of personal and social factors arising from individual characteristics, family, community and school. While some pupils surmount overwhelming debilitating circumstances, others are completely defeated by similar circumstances. One could argue that the former have the gift of personal resilience, but often those pupils who do surmount personal and social difficulties receive the support of at least one mentor who believes in them, and who supports and enables them to succeed.

Schools are concerned about the widespread problem of underachieving pupils, and are striving to develop appropriate school climates in which *all pupils* experience success, are motivated to learn and participate as young citizens in meaningful activities.

With particular regard for able pupils, most schools have appointed a coordinator with responsibility for identifying and monitoring the development of their able pupils. Many schools are developing extension and mentoring programmes so that able pupils can work more independently and build supportive and enabling relationships. In addition, many schools are making links with outside experts so that able pupils can have access to knowledge and expertise of people outside the school.

Hence the analysis of the causes of underachievement of able pupils that follows is not to say that schools are unaware of these issues, but to highlight the challenges that schools are facing. The intention of the analysis outlined below is to instigate discussion and full recognition of the challenges that schools are facing.

Cognition

Different cognitive framework

Some learners have thinking styles that are culturally different from the dominant school culture. This is not to diminish their intellectual ability, but to draw attention to different styles of thinking, such as: different styles of classification; a tendency to prefer divergent rather than convergent modes of thinking; a preference for emotionally based rather than rationally based thinking; a preference for a holistic rather than a segmented approach to learning; a preference for visual rather than verbal thinking, oral rather than written modes, practical rather than 'academic' modes; group-oriented tasks rather than individual activities. While recognising that individuals' thinking styles need to develop across a continuum of these different modes, it is important to recognise the varying predispositions of learners.

Underdeveloped cognitive frameworks

Learners may have a fragmented base of cognitive frameworks even within their own culture; that is, underdeveloped cognitive frameworks caused by lack of appropriate experiential and mediated learning. Teachers need to assess whether the learners have acquired a rich range of basic thinking tools linked with language and emotion as the broad vehicle for learning and communication.

Recent Curriculum Strategy Documents published by the Department for Children, Schools and Families (DCSF) encourage schools to develop a wide range of pedagogical practices that enhance teaching and learning activities across the widest range of cultures, thinking styles and interpersonal interactions.

Language

Underdeveloped first language

Learners may have an 'informal' language that lacks the language tools for formal thinking in school, that is, the logical connectors of complex prepositions for reasoning, the classification language for grouping (comparing similarities and differences), the conjunctions needed for expressing cause and effect and so on.

Bilingual/multilingual learners

If the home language differs from the dominant language used at school, learners could be at a disadvantage since the cognitive demand of continuous translation from one language to another consumes huge mental energy.

'Class' and the dominant language in school

School staff usually use the dominant language of the 'middle class', which is different from many learners' 'working-class' style of language – compounding both of the above points. All educators, but particularly Early Years educators, are concentrating on the development of speaking and listening as the principal foundation for learning.

Culture and values

The dominant school culture

The dominant school culture may be different from the learners' home and community culture. Learners need to bridge both cultures if they are to function effectively in both home and school. This takes enormous courage if it means standing alone within the peer group of street and community.

Many schools are actively celebrating different cultures and are developing positive attitudes to difference and diversity: these developments are not merely token, but form an integral part of school living, sharing and learning.

School versus home

Home values may have short-term, immediate goals (wage earning) rather than long-term goals (further study). Moreover, home values may favour practical skills rather than academic or creative skills.

- Pupil aspirations may be low because of limited family experience, lack of knowledge of career opportunities, lack of confidence, lack of role models who demonstrate high achievement.
- School learning may be perceived as irrelevant to life. In addition, parents may have negative experiences of school themselves and are communicating their own feelings to their children.

However, many schools are concerned to develop good relationships with parents, and the DfES document 'Every Child Matters' seeks to consolidate and extend this liaison between home and school to ensure that learners are safe, healthy, enjoy learning and achieve well, make a positive contribution to school and community life and eventually develop the skills to earn a living in a satisfying way.

School as a centre of excellence

In the drive to raise measurable 'government standards of attainment', schools may concentrate on promoting and celebrating the 'status' subjects of Language, Maths and Science – possibly undervaluing or neglecting to celebrate pupils' multiple capacities across the curriculum.

Thus the challenge to the school is to develop an ethos which actively promotes the belief that pupils are capable of achieving excellence through various modes that are equally valued and celebrated in all subjects across the curriculum. An important part of this ethos is the promotion of personal development as part of the vision of lifelong learning.

Many schools are, indeed, developing excellence across the curriculum as an essential aim of their school development plan, and they are also embracing the concept of excellence across the full range of human capacities. They are demonstrating that by developing pupils' personal achievement, they are also raising standards of attainment.

Personal identity and self-esteem

Self-esteem and self-confidence derive from the positive perception of a personal identity which is supported and celebrated in the learning environment. A negative perception of the self leads to lack of self-confidence and lack of self-worth; this is one of the main causes of underachievement since in a non-supportive environment, pupils can lose their sense of self.

Pupils need to develop an 'internal locus of control' through which they perceive the self as capable, and intelligence as something which can be nurtured and grown, not just celebrated and revered. However, rebuilding students' internal locus of control requires long-term mentoring and support. (See Chapter 2 on the importance of self-esteem and self-confidence.)

Socio-economic

Poverty and sheer practical survival often prevent pupils and their parents/carers from planning ahead. Lack of money management for forward planning, limited goals and the pursuit of immediate gratification are critical factors that impinge on personal career development. Pupils from low socio-economic environments often have limited awareness of their potential for growth and change, and limited knowledge of a full range of career opportunities. Students from ethnic minorities need to feel that they are an integral part of the whole-school population.

In any school, the adolescent peer-group culture exerts a strong influence to conform to the perceptions, perceived status and values of the majority who perceive themselves as remaining within their current life situations. Changing this school culture needs a whole-school ethos that celebrates excellence both *across* and *outside* the curriculum.

Parental support

Many parents have negative associations with school and a lack of knowledge of the current system, and hence lack the confidence to approach the school with possible concerns. Often they do not have the knowledge and experience to discuss long-term goals, and do not have the understanding of the need for long-term support. However, many schools are building bridges and encouraging parents to be involved in decision-making, cultural activities and educational programmes in school.

Peer-group pressure

After the family, peer-group pressure is a major contributing factor to underachievement. Peer-group pressure in our current society often conveys a strong message that it is 'not cool to be bright'; street language is perceived as the only acceptable 'lingo'; there is widespread misuse of drugs and alcohol; and early sexual experiences are regarded as the norm. In what has been called our 'value-less society', school often represents an 'alien' culture that students reject in favour of immediate tangible goals and leisure activities that they regard as necessary and pleasurable.

Lack of challenge in the curriculum

Lack of appropriate depth and breadth, lack of relevance to life and overload of content in the everyday curriculum constitute the major causes of the underachievement of many pupils; providing differentiation of learning experiences constitutes teachers' greatest professional challenge. A class of thirty pupils presents a huge spectrum of needs that is extremely daunting for a single teacher, but when curriculum teams plan together within and across subject areas the burden of time needed for planning is lightened. The original case-study research (2006–2007) highlighted a number of pupil observations about the lack of challenge in their learning experiences and activities. Box 1.4 summarises their observations. (See Chapter 4 on the importance of challenge and Chapter 5 on students as researchers.)

Box 1.4 Lack of challenge for more able learners

Many able learners:

- perceive lack of relevance and challenge in the school curriculum;
- are required to memorise facts rather than tackle issues within an active problem-solving scenario;
- lack opportunities for learning through real-life experience;
- repeat skills and content already mastered;
- lack ownership, negotiation and decision-making in their learning;
- lack recognition of personal skills and strengths;
- lack opportunities for leadership experience.

How do we overcome the syndrome of underachievement?

The concept map at the end of this chapter (see page 30) summarises the following section and can be used as the basis for reflective staff dis-cussion with regard to what the school is already doing well and what practices need to be developed or extended. In addition, the writers of this text extend all the points in the concept map within their chapters, so it is a good idea if staff read each chapter that is relevant to the intended discussion.

As always, when we are dealing with the complexity and diversity of human nature – especially of young still-maturing people – there are no straightforward or quick-fix answers. And over recent years, many slick, quick-fix, often costly, solutions have certainly been propounded. Very often these quick-fix solutions are like pieces of sticking plaster that try to hide the deeply engrained developmental wounds, but they fail to diagnose and tackle the deep initial *causes* of the wounds. All teachers (and parents/carers) know that any change in human behaviours and attitudes takes time: the brain must unlearn undesirable patterns of response and relearn desirable ones. Throughout our lives, the emotional centre of the brain very quickly and deeply absorbs and responds to messages emanating from the environment and the attitudes of others, and any healing and consequent regrowth is a long-term matter – certainly not a quick-fix matter.

Self-esteem and self-belief, once destroyed or diminished, require intensive mentoring and support before the individual is fully renewed and revitalised to full functioning capacity. Underachievement so easily becomes a chronic syndrome requiring a huge turn-around in personal motivation, response habits and attitudes. And this is certainly not easy when significant gaps in learning have developed over time. If there are any 'quick-fixes' around that would make a real, lasting difference, then we can be sure that caring teachers and parents/carers, as well as the learners themselves, would grab the opportunity!

The case-study research of twelve schools (2006–2007) highlighted characteristics of schools that have successfully dealt with potential underachievement. No school embodied and practised every possible remediating, empowering strategy, but every school in the study practised a significant core of enabling educational philosophies and practices that had been developed systematically across the whole school over a number of years. Certainly, no school propounded 'quick-fix' solutions: every school talked about their development as on-going democratic growth managed, encouraged and sustained over several years.

Crucially, the major strategies that emerged from the case-study schools are presented in the following sections.

Visionary, energetic, distributed leadership

- The senior management team (SMT) are practical 'hands-on' educators who learners see around the school on a daily basis; and they can address pupils by name, knowing the background of pupils' successes and special needs. At primary level, this is obviously easier because the school populations are smaller, but at secondary level, the management teams work together closely as a complex interrelated unit comprising senior management, heads of year, subject leaders and teachers with special responsibilities. Despite time pressures, they *make the time* to communicate with the whole teaching body, parents, pupils, support staff and governors. The headteachers see themselves primarily as communicators and facilitators and not as administrators shut away in ivory towers in the administration block.

- Both primary and secondary schools maintain that the time spent in communicating and sharing establishes the school's ethos of caring for individuals and creates a real sense of a school community where everyone matters and has a real voice. In interview, members of these inclusive school communities express their feelings of being valued members of a dynamic team, and the feeling of ownership and participation in all decision-making is clearly evident throughout each school. The schools maintain that strong communication networks enable the personalisation of learning and teaching to become a reality, and make it easier to recognise symptoms of underachievement and other special needs.

- In every one of the case-study schools, the pupil voice is strong and real, and has considerable influence on both school decisions and issues of personal development. Pupils are encouraged to express their views and to feel they are in partnership with their teachers. Pupils do not perceive that 'education is done to them'; they feel they are an essential part of the process. They feel confident that they can discuss any aspect of their schooling with both teachers and the senior management team. Learning is personalised and carefully monitored; pupils are excited about learning, highly motivated and proud of their achievements. They perceive that teachers' expectations of their achievements are high and they respond to this positively. The pupils are trusted and expected to reflect on their learning experiences, and careers' advice is rich and developed early with a sense of vision and entitlement. The major emphasis across the curriculum is placed on activities that encourage problem-solving and thinking skills, self-assessment and self-monitoring skills, questioning, efficient recording and research skills.

- In line with promoting a community involvement in the school, communication avenues with the outside world are carefully fostered and are open and clearly accessible. Parents/carers feel that they have open access to the school and that they can approach any member of the senior management or member of staff if they need to discuss an issue; they are very much involved in school activities and are consulted and kept informed about all school policy and intended future development. They have a sense of both ownership and partnership and are proud of the school's efforts and achievements. In some of the case-study schools, where, initially, many parents seldom or never crossed the barriers of the school gates, involving parents and carers has meant that huge amounts of time and care has been put into persuading parents that a school is a welcoming and friendly place where they can express their thoughts, worries and feelings. We need to remember that for many parents, their schools were places of failure and loss of self-esteem. It is obvious that they will not readily return to the school situation unless they feel welcomed and at ease.

- Importantly, governors also have a strong voice and are fully aware of their school's developmental plans and practice and are active supporters. Many governors spend time in the schools during the day, working in classrooms and talking with teachers and pupils. Those who are unable to do this make sure that they attend all school meetings and functions. All governors feel they have a responsibility to their community and their school; they are committed citizens and proud of their work with the school.

Posts of special responsibility

- Teachers undertaking roles with special responsibilities are always included in the senior management team (SMT) on the basis that they have detailed knowledge of the individual pupils in their special care and are, consequently, perceived as having a critical influence in all decision-making. For example, meeting the needs of pupils who are 'statemented' or on a special needs register, or who are working in their second language, runs alongside the needs of potentially able pupils: the wide spectrum of these pupils' needs are integrated alongside the needs of all other pupils. Some of these teachers are, indeed, young in the profession, but they are considered as key people alongside more experienced members of staff. There is no sense of differential 'status' but there a strong sense of shared community. In particular, any discussion of what best practice might be for some individuals is seen as having relevance for *all* pupils.
- The staff holding posts of special responsibility also includes lead teachers who demonstrate high-level teaching skills and high-level leadership skills, and so are able to inspire confidence amongst teachers, pupils and parents. They are responsible for implementing, evaluating and monitoring aspects of the school improvement plans, and they have a firm grasp of their roles and responsibilities. However, pupils are also closely involved in evaluating the relevance and suitability of their general school experiences and their specific learning targets. After all, pupils are the receiving clients and they can clearly, and sometimes vociferously, express their thoughts and feelings if they are given the chance! All pupils certainly do know if their educational experiences are working for them! All the case-study schools have a well-developed strategy for in-service staff development, and updating this programme arises naturally from the pupil review sessions where not only are the needs of pupils identified but also staff and the whole school needs. Here agendas are raised and targets set and built into the school development plan.
- All the primary schools belong to their local Primary Learning Network, a cluster group of schools who work together for the common good of the cluster. Where appropriate, the cluster includes the local secondary

school; however, some secondary schools receive pupils from such a wide range of primary schools that this precludes them from belonging to a particular primary cluster. In cluster meetings, there is the sense of working together to share good practice, to discuss challenges and to build cooperative initiatives for development. In some schools, lead teachers are encouraged to visit other schools in the cluster to demonstrate strategies for best practice. The intense competition that characterised so many schools several years ago has been replaced with cooperation and mutual support, and one could argue that 'humanity' is being put back into schools with people being considered before numbers and tables.

- Depending on pupils' needs, aims vary in the focus directed towards raising achievement. Some schools produce a pupil pro-forma for Assessment and Review of Learning. It comprises a column for pupils' strengths and needs in the autumn term; a review column at the beginning of the spring term and a box to write the agreed forward targets; followed by late spring and summer reviews to consider progress and future needs. It would be difficult for any child's needs at any level to escape this thorough and expert ongoing diagnosis of needs. Staff believe that the time taken to complete these pro-formas, which always involves discussion with the pupils, is one of the important strategies that prevents underachievement.

- Secondary departments are also additionally responsible for monitoring the progress of all students within their subject areas, but especially those with Individual Education Plans (IEPs). Quality leadership and knowledge of individual pupils are, once again, the keys to developing worthwhile and motivating provision. In past years, there has been too great an emphasis on the superficial ticking of boxes and filling in of forms with numbers that can be manipulated into desirable statistics, and less emphasis on the essential humanity of educational interaction backed by discourse and caring. In the case-study schools, there is great emphasis on pupil, parent and teacher relationships with home agreements drawn up that highlight both the learners' needs and the parental responsibilities. This agreement respects the pupils' home language and culture and is translated into the often many different languages within the school.

- The case-study schools engage in self-assessment against the National Quality Standards (NQS) and/or the NACE Challenge Award in order to review their plans, to set new targets each year and to report back to the appropriate person who discusses what further steps are to be taken. (Chapter 6 on organisation and leadership highlights particularly the effective use of the NACE Challenge Award.)

Recognition of gifts and talents

- With regard to identifying pupils' gifts and talents, a carefully fostered inclusive ethos exists throughout each case-study school, based on the premise that the school needs to *create* opportunities that will enable *all* pupils to *discover* their potentials. The living philosophy that lies at the foundation of each school is that a school can create pupils who have gifts and talents through a wide range of curricular and 'out-of-hours' activities. The emphasis is on celebrating and giving equal status to *all* learners' potentials and achievements, and it runs right across the full spectrum of human capacities: social, emotional, spiritual, visual/spatial, mechanical/technical, physical/movement, auditory/musical, scientific, linguistic (oral and written) and mathematical. But enabling pupils to discover their gifts and talents is not sufficient: these gifts and talents not only need recognition, but also support, extension opportunities and celebration.

- Discovering and celebrating all pupils' potentials relies heavily on the perceptive and sensitive high-level skills needed for qualitative assessment through regular staff and pupil discussions, the provision of open-ended challenges for pupils, pupil peer- and self-referrals, parental referrals and, importantly, intensive continuing professional development (CPD) that hones teachers' observation and assessment skills. In schools that celebrate all pupils' gifts across the full spectrum of human capacities, teachers, parents, pupils and governors need to be fully aware that this is embedded in the whole-school policy; and that the school perceives that 'intelligence' is a combination of academic, creative and practical abilities.

- This broad concept of intelligence is not fixed in any individual, and all pupils are capable of growth and change. It is empowering and motivating for pupils to realise that they are capable of learning, developing *and* succeeding within their strongest capacities: this provides the essential motivation needed to persevere in developing those capacities that may be weaker. When schools accept the vast amount of cognitive research that indicates that the concept of 'intelligence' is centred around problem-solving and thinking skills and that these strategies can be taught, then the processes of teaching and learning become increasingly dynamic and enabling both for teachers and pupils. When pupils believe that they have worth and they can improve and succeed; this belief in the self as a dynamic, growing person is another key to preventing the syndrome of underachieving and disillusioned learners.

- Although teacher perception and qualitative procedures for assessment are of primary importance, schools also use a variety of testing strategies that are quantitative; and these include appropriate verbal and non-verbal group tests, SATs levels, class tests and examination results. However, these kinds of test results yield a measurement that is derived from 'correct' answers. One cannot be creative with questions that require 'right' answers and, consequently, innovative answers that lie beyond the 'marking scheme' are marked 'wrong'.

•   Quantitative tests can be used to good effect when employed diagnostically to ascertain a pupil's level of competence across a range of skills and knowledge needed for 'formal' school learning. Also, they are useful to compare performance across an age group on a range of skills necessary for school learning. When a pupil scores highly on a non-verbal test and much lower on a verbal test, this can be an indicator of underachievement. The following Boxes 1.5 and 1.6 show the commonly used pupil assessment procedures in the case-study schools, with regard to identifying potential gifts and talents and also special needs. As stated above, sensitive interpretation of the quantitative tests can be strong indicators of underachievement.

Box 1.5 Assessment and identification procedures used (inter alia) at primary level

1   At Early Years and Foundation levels, the quality of teacher observation is considered of primary importance, with the emphasis on identifying pupil progress from their base-line assessment on entry. The emphasis is on providing learners with rich opportunities for experiential learning and interaction across the Learning Areas.

2   As learners progress, teacher assessment through tracking continues using a local authority model; National Curriculum levelling and target setting for individuals and groups; test results using the Standardised Attainment Tests (SATs statutory and optional); and NFER non-verbal and verbal reasoning tests. In Years 4 and 5 Cognitive Ability Tests are administered. The Target Tracker package is also used. Continuous monitoring of attainment, observation on the curriculum task, observations and results from extended opportunities and partner projects are key strategies.

3   An important emphasis is given to qualitative procedures throughout the primary stage: a comprehensive picture is built up of each child's progress and performance by a rigorous process of continuous assessment through observation, careful record keeping and collation of evidence including samples of pupils' work, discussion with colleagues, pupils and parents/carers.

4 Evidence from all these sources is used in regular pupil review processes to ensure that the provision is effective, inclusive and individualised, and that the support offered meets the needs of all the children. These processes also engage staff in a continuous cycle of self-reflection and development. Any discrepancy between a pupil's targets and performance is investigated, and appropriate intervention is diagnosed and agreed with the pupil.

5 The assessment coordinator, G + T coordinator, SENCO and class teachers carry out testing on individual pupils as necessary.

Box 1.6 Assessment and identification procedures used (inter alia) at secondary level

1 All the secondary schools in the research study maintain close links with the feeder primary schools, and primary records are fully investigated. Pupils complete forms detailing their interests before arriving in Year 7.

2 To assess attainment and progress, schools use standardised test results: SATs on entry; MIDYIS tests for Year 7; SATs for Key Stage 3; YELLIS for Year 10 and ALIS for Year 12; Cognitive Ability Tests – a score of 126 or above in one battery or 120 or above in two batteries; Level 8 in Mathematics or a Level 8 teacher assessment; UK Maths Challenge – Gold Award. GCSE results are also used – a points score of 58 or above in the best eight subjects (where A*= 8, A=7, B=6 etc).

3 Teacher observation in a particular subject is considered vital to the identification process, especially where perceived potential is not demonstrated in assessment scores. Mentors play an important role in this procedure. Also evidence of outstanding achievement in an academic or creative arts activity pursued outside school is considered; for example, success in a national-level chess or debating competition or outstanding performance in a master-class, Aimhigher or a gifted and talented programme.

Continuity of educational experiences: transition and transfer

- Pupil progress is monitored from the base-line point of entry. Individual Education Plans (IEPs) and the open-ended G + T register are regularly reviewed and then transferred between the phases. This is helped by each school's highly efficient system of collecting, collating and analysing data on pupil progress.

- There is excellent liaison between the schools at every stage of transition through detailed reports of pupils' achievements regarding in-school and out-of-school activities, examples of pupils' work and both quantitative and qualitative comments on pupils' strengths and areas needing support. These reports are made available to, and discussed by, all staff so that repetition of skills and mastery of knowledge is avoided. Thus, staff are aware of pupils' levels of achievement and the spectrum of special needs before they arrive in the next phase: this enables teachers to do forward planning to address individual needs, building upon the profiles of information that pupils have acquired prior to and after arrival. The transition profiles inform group and individual lesson planning and schemes of work.

- Designated staff carry specific responsibilities for data acquisition, the security of this and the dissemination to all staff. Vitally, this data is maintained and updated on a weekly or two-weekly basis, and staff are expected to cooperate in keeping this data active and alive. Extensive school IT facilities support this network, and time is saved by using an efficient communication system. Transition booklets, examples of work, induction days and computer data transfer are characteristic of all the case-study schools.

- Alive, active communication channels also exist between universities, secondary and primary schools, and some Year 11, 12 and 13 pupils engage in work placements in primary schools, supervising various activities and mentoring programmes. In turn, secondary pupils have access to tutors and mentors from universities. The ethos is that of cooperation, flexibility and sharing for the benefit of the learners,

- Many schools across the country have taken on the responsibility of mentoring parents. During the phases of Foundation, Early Years and Key Stages 1 and 2, the case-study schools provide regular classes for parents according to their needs. The classes range from suggestions for play activities to healthy eating suggestions and include sessions whereby parents have the opportunity to understand the principles of best practice for primary education. In addition, at secondary level, the schools in the research study make sure that parents are well-informed in matters such as career opportunities and the necessary qualification requirements; they endeavour to 'dispel the mystery' of tertiary education presenting university study as the right of every student to access post-secondary education.

Prevention of potential underachievement

- Differentiated provision is perceived as integral to whole-school planning: the curriculum is the result of negotiation of areas for study. The emphasis is on students constructing knowledge and meanings for themselves, rather than merely the dispensing of set, immutable content in the well-known Freire 'banking' concept of filling up empty minds. Planning is expected to show coherent levels of increasing complexity and is not just a selection of extra exercises for the 'early finishers'.

- Importantly, independent study and research are key characteristics of negotiated learning goals. Differentiation for the more able is targeted on offering more cognitive challenge to develop problem-solving and thinking skills, higher-order thinking and questioning skills. Extra support for those pupils who need it is carefully organised especially through teaching assistants who are well trained. Collaborative, net-worked e-learning is well advanced and being constantly extended.

- The pupils are well involved in the formal decision-making processes in the school. There are regular class council meetings, school council meetings and a headteacher's suggestion box. Vitally, the pupil voice is significant and is heard and taken into account. Pupils know that their views matter and make a difference, and so they participate in all school matters – a wonderful experience that generates lifelong commitment, self-confidence and active involvement in workplace and community affairs.

- Teaching *and* non-teaching staff receive planned and in-depth continuing professional development (CPD) with regard to: continuous and systematic differentiation of learning activities; problem-solving and thinking skills and higher-order questioning, with guidance on how to implement these into lesson planning; accommodation of different learning styles and capacities; and assessment (both formative and summative). The continuing development of the school staff is exactly that – a continuing carefully planned sequence of relevant development seminars and activities to increase theoretical and practical understanding of the constituents of best practice.

- All schools provide an extensive range of out-of-hours learning opportunities: some pupils are guided to participate, but the activities are open to any pupil who shows an interest. This is regarded as another avenue for the identification of pupil potential and is in line with the philosophy of 'identification through provision'.

- Throughout the year, the schools make extensive use of both qualitative and quantitative data to evaluate new developments and to evaluate the effectiveness of different learning experiences for particular groups of students. Each school's *Handbook of Policy and Practice* provides extensive guidance on how to differentiate learning tasks, and each secondary subject department is responsible for outlining the strategies that are used to ensure that each student is working at the appropriate level.

- Schools are expected to self-assess against National Quality Standards and the NACE Challenge Award, and they do this through an audit that constantly refines their procedures. Staff have a clear view of procedures, the ownership of responsibilities, and what is expected of them. The National Curriculum Framework is personalised in terms of day-to-day teaching and the production of regular progress reports and target setting with pupils at least once a term. This is where underachievement is addressed. Staff look very closely at any discrepancy between a pupil's targets and current performance. If a pupil is underperforming, there is serious conversation that attempts to identify a good intervention such as finding a mentor, examining the problems within the work, or altering expectations or work styles. There is also a very close review of schemes of work within years and departments.

- Year and department teams, plus every teacher, are challenged to see that individual pupils are set realistic, contractual and negotiated performance targets that personalise the learning; they identify who takes responsibility and they guarantee a conversation that reviews progress and addresses complications. This procedure sets the landscape and the architecture of the relationships that drive education. The processes feel creative and nurturing, and independent thinking is fostered in order to support the development of personal identity. The students feel empowered and motivated as major stakeholders rather than as passive school attenders or passengers. Everyone has a personal challenge and the opportunity to succeed across a very wide range of activities in and outside of school.

- When underachievement is identified, an initial meeting between the pupil and the teacher begins the learning conversation. The outcome of this interaction might result in a new approach to learning, new avenues of support from staff, peers and families, new work and homework strategies and incentives, new expectations, new targets and the booking of further meetings as and when necessary. Parents/Carers can become involved when necessary but the emphasis is upon nurturing the independence of the pupil, encouraging the pupil to make a personal commitment to agreed targets. The pupil is also encouraged to keep a personal portfolio of progress and self-assessment. The ethos behind all interactions is that schools exist *for* pupils rather than as places that pupils have to attend.

- Sometimes it has to be acknowledged that the cause of some under-achievement can lie within personal circumstances outside the control of the school. Many pupils are grossly disadvantaged by their home circumstances and street peer-group environment. Without prolonged help and support, these problems can overwhelm an individual and in these cases counselling is available both within the school and externally.

- If the syndrome of underachievement is pervasive throughout a phase or a class/subject group, rather than an individual occurrence, then the relevant staff collaboratively and very bravely face this head on. They look to group solutions such as reorganising schedules of work, raising expectations, lowering anxieties, revisiting year and departmental policies and resources and providing staff training and, if necessary, personal staff support. The staff take proactive measures to prevent or minimise underachievement *before* it happens. The SMT are constantly assessing the impact of all school policies with vulnerable pupils and they take preventative action where it is felt to be warranted. This is reflected in the annual construction of the school development plan. The prevailing school message conveyed to the children and young people is that staff believe in the potential of all their pupils and want them to succeed. In many cases, the school and the teachers provide the only place where learners feel secure and valued.

- Pupils value negotiating their learning and development journeys with staff and respond to the encouragement to use their own initiative for decision-making. What they think and believe in terms of their own self-concept, self-assessments, critical reflections and target settings lay the essential foundation for sustained effort towards further achievement.

Assessment for Learning

- The National Curriculum Framework (England) is intended to provide guidelines for the development of a spiral curriculum that extends in each key phase. Consequently, there is considerable repetition of the same content in each phase of the guidance framework. Consequently, a major challenge for all teachers is to assess what pupils already know and understand *before* they begin to plan activities for further and extended learning. Assessment for learning necessitates systematic pre-assessment strategies, careful record keeping and close liaison with the learners' previous teachers, then effective planning can avoid repetition of skills and knowledge already mastered. Challenge is then presented through high-quality, open-ended tasks so that there is always differentiated work and extension material available. By assessing performance on these tasks it is then possible to set individuals even more challenging targets. Through the differentiation, extension and enrichment strategies in lessons, teachers are able to use curriculum-based assessment to extend the pupils' range of skills and to further develop the cognitive stretch in targeting thinking and questioning skills.

- In all the case-study schools, pupils are allowed to make choices about their areas of study and then to choose how they will organise their own work. They are expected to carry out, unaided, tasks that stretch their capabilities and help develop their abilities to evaluate and check their work. Pupils set their own targets and monitor their own progress through self-assessment and marking each other's work. The skills of the teachers lie in assessing what information, skills and strategies the learners already have and what further development they need to carry out their learning tasks.

- Schools using the TASC Problem-Solving Framework as a major strategy to addressing able pupils' needs have developed an assessment and monitoring profile that provides qualitative as well as quantifiable outcomes: staff feel that the TASC Problem-Solving process that broadly scaffolds independent learning, allows them to have greater freedom to observe pupils.

- At secondary level, a two-year Key Stage 3 programme and a Year 9 creative curriculum came about as a result of staff talking to students about their learning. Pupils expressed their frustration with the high level of repetition at Key Stage 3. Many other changes have resulted from discussions between G + T students and the coordinator, which are then shared with other teachers and departments.

- Through the power of being given ownership of their learning paths and opportunities to monitor their own progress, pupils attribute success and failure to their own decision-making rather than blaming other factors such as the teachers or the curriculum. Pupils value opportunities to negotiate with staff and to use their own initiative: what they think and believe in terms of their own self-assessments, critical reflections and target settings predominate. These conversations take place on both a formal and an informal basis; and what the school staff provide in the way of qualitative and quantitative data to inform these conversations is appreciated. There are also opportunities for pupils to take responsibility to repair conversations with teachers when somehow the discussions are not achieving the potential that was perceived.

- The purpose of all assessment is to show personal progression within each subject, or group of subjects, and this information is shared with pupils and parents/carers. Pupil self-assessment powerfully complements other types of assessment and encourages students to carry personal responsibility for their progress. Teachers use both Assessment for Learning (formative assessment) and Assessment of Learning (summative assessment). Written commentaries in pupils' books provide evidence of personalised learning through comments about possible avenues for improvement under the influence of AfL principles. The emphasis is on positive *feed-forward* comments that learners can use for reflection and further learning.

- Teachers see assessing work with carefully orchestrated *feed-forward* to pupils as a key opportunity to ask more high-level questions that probe for a better understanding of what a given pupil has learned and where perhaps the pupil might need specific tuition. They see close links between AfL and the promotion of the National Quality Standards (NQS) and NACE Challenge Award (C/A) in education.

Conclusion

It is evident that schools are facing huge challenges in education arising from a complex network of powerful social, economic and political influences. Yet many schools are still providing high-quality education even though many learners are manifesting personal needs that completely exhaust teachers in their day-to-day nurturing care of young people. In the case-study schools, school personnel can produce evidence of high-level, caring leadership and senior management; they recognise the power and the demand of personalising learning and are accommodating the diverse needs of all learners; they retain the vision that they entered the teaching profession in order to inspire and lead young people to discover their gifts and talents and to prepare them for lifelong learning.

This chapter summarises a wide range of successful learning, teaching and organisational strategies that have been developed in the twelve original case-study schools. Ongoing chapters extend this summary and provide greater depth and breadth to the concepts outlined here, including both theory and practice.

In essence the case-study schools are developing a creative curriculum overflowing with opportunities whereby learners are given the chance to discover their potential gifts and talents. The schools have become the centres of learners' lives – a place where they feel safe and happy and can have dreams and visions for their future. In addition, the schools have become a focus for community healing, drawing in parents and governors as partners in the education of the young. Teachers have become mentors and facilitators not only for young peoples' learning but for the development of their fulfilling and productive lives.

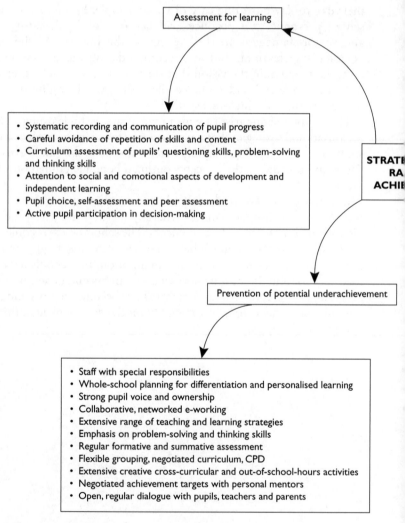

Assessment for learning

- Systematic recording and communication of pupil progress
- Careful avoidance of repetition of skills and content
- Curriculum assessment of pupils' questioning skills, problem-solving and thinking skills
- Attention to social and comotional aspects of development and independent learning
- Pupil choice, self-assessment and peer assessment
- Active pupil participation in decision-making

STRAT
RA
ACHI

Prevention of potential underachievement

- Staff with special responsibilities
- Whole-school planning for differentiation and personalised learning
- Strong pupil voice and ownership
- Collaborative, networked e-working
- Extensive range of teaching and learning strategies
- Emphasis on problem-solving and thinking skills
- Regular formative and summative assessment
- Flexible grouping, negotiated curriculum, CPD
- Extensive creative cross-curricular and out-of-school-hours activities
- Negotiated achievement targets with personal mentors
- Open, regular dialogue with pupils, teachers and parents

Figure 1.1 Summary concept map 1

- Delegated but shared responsibility
- Influence of Lead Teachers
- Close primary – secondary cluster liaison
- Continuous assessment of pupil progress
- National Quality Standards and NACE Challenge Award
- Continuous monitoring of CPD

- Practical, hands-on leadership
- Shared communication
- Ethos of inclusive community
- Strong pupil and parent/governor voice – ownership
- Personalised learning
- Ethos of celebration of effort

Posts of special responsibility

Visionary, distributed leadership

ES FOR
NG
EMENT

Transition and transfer

- Regular monitoring of individual achievement
- Regular sharing of pupil progress
- Avoidance of repetition of skills and content
- Close communication with other phases, parents, schools

Recognition of gifts and talents

- Creative curriculum of opportunity
- Qualitative teacher/pupil observation
- Celebration of spectrum of human capacities
- Diagnostic use of quantitative testing
- Careful monitoring of potential underachievement

References and further reading

Wallace, B. (2008a) 'A vision of Paulo Freire's philosophy: understanding his essential dynamism of learning and teaching', in Shaughnessy, M. Galligan, E. and Hurtado de Vivas, R. (eds) *Pioneers in Education: Essays in Honor of Paulo Freire*. New York: Nova Science Publishers Inc.

Wallace, B. (2008b) (ed.) *Gifted Education International* Vol 24 Nos 2 and 3. Oxford: AB Academic Publishers.

Wallace, B. (2003) *Using History to Develop Thinking Skills at Key Stage 2*. London: David Fulton Publishers (A NACE-Fulton Pub.).

Wallace, B. (2002) *Teaching Thinking Skills Across the Early Years*. London: David Fulton Publishers (A NACE-Fulton Pub.).

Wallace, B. (2002) *Teaching Thinking Skills Across the Middle Years*. London: David Fulton Publishers (A NACE-Fulton Pub.).

Wallace, B. (2001) *Teaching Thinking Skills Across the Primary Curriculum*. London: David Fulton Publishers (A NACE-Fulton Pub.).

Wallace, B. and Eriksson, G. (eds) (2006) *Diversity in Gifted Education: International Perspectives on Global Issues*. London: Routledge.

Wallace, B., Cave, D. and Berry, A. (2008) *Teaching Problem-Solving and Thinking Skills through Science*. London: Routledge.

Wallace, B., Maker, J. and Cave, D. (2004) *Thinking Skills and Problem-Solving: An Inclusive Approach*. London: David Fulton Publishers (A NACE-Fulton Pub.).

Wallace, B., Fitton, S., Leyden, S., Montgomery, D., Pomerantz, M. and Winstanley, C. (2007) *Raising the Achievement of Able, Gifted and Talented Pupils within an Inclusive School Framework: Guidelines for schools to audit and extend existing best practice*. Oxford: National Association for Able Children in Education. publications@nace.co.uk.

Chapter 2

Social and emotional needs of gifted and talented underachievers

Sue Leyden

Pride, passion and success is the experience we hope for every learner.
(Headteacher, Portswood Primary School)

Introduction

The social and emotional needs of children and young people should be at the heart of educational thinking. Children who are unhappy or unsettled do not flourish in school. They are unlikely to make best use of their learning experiences and most probably will underachieve. This chapter looks at the key factors that underpin successful social and emotional development as well as personal fulfilment, with special reference to potential high flyers.

The first part of the chapter provides a theoretical basis for looking at social and emotional needs as children grow towards adulthood. We then consider some important factors that may present problems for children whose development marks them out as different. This is followed by an examination of successful educational practice in supporting the social and emotional well-being of potentially gifted and talented children, drawn from the experience of members of the research team and witnessed in the twelve schools that took part in the research project. The final section provides practical examples of engaging children in constructive discussions about their work, their hopes and needs, that help them plan how to become more successful learners, performers and members of the community. Where illustrative examples and quotations from children are provided, names and details have been changed to ensure confidentiality is respected.

Understanding social and emotional needs

We are all social and emotional beings. From our earliest moments we experience what it is to be cared for by others and gradually discover for ourselves the importance and value of caring for others. It is through these reciprocal relationships within our family, our friendships and our communities, that we develop a sense of ourselves as social individuals with a valued contribution to make as members of the wider society in which we live, learn, work and play.

Feeling secure as an individual, with a healthy awareness of our place in the community, is at the heart of our relationships with others. We all need to learn how to get along with others, to enjoy their company. We need to feel that not only do we belong but also that we have a valued presence and contribution to make to our family, friends and the wider community.

Maslow's (1954) diagrammatic conceptualisation of the process (Figure 2.1) made an instant impact on our thinking and understanding of human growth, development and motivation. It is still widely used in many social, educational, industrial and organisational settings.

Whilst most of us may share these common needs or experiences on our path to personal self-fulfilment, we also recognise some will struggle more than others on the journey. For instance, feeling good about oneself is an essential component of our social and emotional well-being. But children whose emotional development is in any way impaired or neglected, or who lack the experience of being loved and belonging, may struggle to develop these crucial feelings of self-worth or constructive self-esteem.

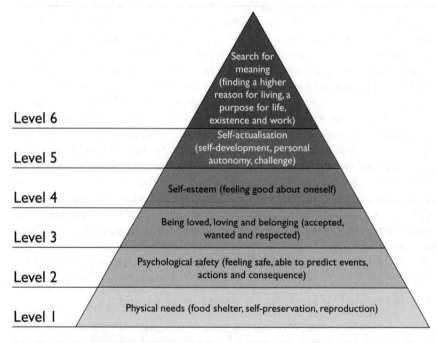

Figure 2.1 Maslow's 'Hierarchy of Needs' (1954)

Growing up gifted and talented

'Being labelled "gifted" has been the bane of my life' said one young person in Joan Freeman's longitudinal study, *Gifted Children Growing Up* (Freeman, 1991). Freeman, who tracked the development of a large number of children identified as 'gifted', described the difficulties some of them had experienced as they moved through childhood and adolescence. Other studies have also found that there can be problems for children who have abilities and talents that make them stand out or appear to be different from their peers.

Whilst the majority of able and talented children in the studies were managing well, some had found it hard to make friends from a very early age. They had lost interest in doing the things others of their age were doing, or had become frustrated by not being able to hold discussions at a level that interested them. They were finding they had little in common with children of their own age, yet were not accepted by groups of older children.

In school many of the children had found the work too easy. They felt bored and irritated at being 'held back', and wanted to spend more time on topics that interested them. They saw little point in work they found to be either repetitive or routine. Others had never had to make an effort to produce work of a high standard. Therefore, they either developed an unrealistic notion of their abilities that would cause them problems in the future, or had not been able to develop effective learning habits. Jocelyn Lavin, who had shown exceptional intellectual ability and musical talent throughout her school years, recalls: 'Everything came too easily for me at school' (*Guardian*, 20 December 2008). When, at university, she found for the first time there was something she could not do, her whole sense of self-worth was shaken.

There can be other consequences of growing up 'gifted'. Precocious children may regard themselves as 'special', and perhaps more important and 'better' than others. They may adopt an arrogant stance which others find off-putting. Or they may protect their self-esteem by concentrating on developing their own interests and skills at the expense of social relationships. Others may seek to gain attention and recognition in other ways, such as playing the fool, causing disruption or buying their way into a group.

Teachers, too, may find it difficult to accommodate an unusually able child in their class, especially if that child is demanding, challenging or unwilling to take part in the activities that have been planned. Teachers are only human! They can feel personally and professionally challenged by both the child and, sometimes, the child's parents.

It may not be easy to help a child find friends and feel welcome in the class. But all children need friends. A child without friends is likely to be an unhappy child. A child without friends will be a child at risk. A child who feels unhappy or unwelcome is unlikely to benefit from the learning opportunities the school provides.

Much has changed since Joan Freeman undertook her research. The project that led to the writing of this book provided ample evidence as to just how significant these changes have been. In her opening chapter, Belle Wallace has described the many examples of excellent and innovative practice in the way teaching and learning takes place and the opportunities that are available to all children, whatever their talents and abilities. The requirement on schools to specifically include the needs of their most able and talented pupils in all aspects of school planning and provision has led to many interesting and exciting developments in the curriculum as well as in the opportunities available out of school. The emphasis now given to monitoring the progress and welfare of each and every child in the school means that teachers have become more aware of the problems that some gifted and talented pupils face. Monitoring arrangements through regular reviews with pupils have helped identify and highlight those personal and relationship difficulties that may blight a pupil's life and put constraints on their development.

In her chapter, Belle Wallace has discussed the many potential causes of underachievement. These can, of course, affect any child, regardless of their ability. However, children of high potential may be more susceptible than others to particular situations that can have a negative impact on their development and well-being, such as low expectations (or lack of appropriate challenge), fear of failure and negative peer pressure.

Low expectations

Despite the exciting developments in teaching and learning that have taken place, the abilities and potential of very able and talented pupils can still be underestimated. Low expectations at any stage in a child's time in school can lead to that child becoming complacent and therefore unwilling to make much effort. Such children may learn to be what Belle Wallace has termed 'complacent conformers', or hidden underachievers. Michael Buscemi describes such a situation perfectly in his wonderful poem, 'The Average Child':

> I don't cause teachers trouble,
> My grades have been okay.
> I listen in my classes.
> I'm in school every day.
>
> My teachers think I'm average,
> My parents think so too.
> I wish I didn't know that, though,
> There's lots I'd like to do.
>
> I'd like to build a rocket,
> I read a book on how.

Or start a stamp collection . . .
But no use trying now.

'Cause, since I found I'm average,
I'm smart enough you see
To know there's nothing special
I should expect of me.

I'm part of that majority,
That hump part of the bell,
Who spends his life unnoticed
In an average kind of hell.

(First presented at the 1979 National PTA Convention
by Michael Buscemi, Quest International)

There are many different pathways to learning. It is unrealistic to expect every lesson of every day to be full of excitement and challenge. But teaching that is unimaginative or lacks appropriate intellectual challenge is likely to lead to a child becoming frustrated, losing interest in taking part in class activities, switched off or antagonistic to school. This can have devastating long-term consequences on a child's academic progress and social development. The child may fail to develop good working routines and so may never 'learn how to learn'.

As was the case with Jocelyn Lavin, lack of suitable challenge can also result in children developing an unrealistic and unhealthy understanding of their abilities. They always expect to do well, to achieve high grades, to be top of the class, to be recognised as a success. Their belief in themselves as high performers becomes so embedded in their self-concept, such a fundamental part of what they think of as 'me', that they feel dismayed when they are unable to solve a problem or to achieve the standard they had come to expect.

David is the youngest son in a family of high achievers. His home life is full of adventure and exciting opportunities. Whilst his parents are also high achievers themselves, they are more interested in their son's all-round development than his achieving academic success, and they encourage him to pursue his own interests. Sadly, in school, David is bored. Aged 6, he described his time in the infant school as a 'life sentence'! His performance on NFER Ability tests did not suggest particularly high ability, but, as he explains, he had not seen any purpose in taking the tests seriously. In Junior school he is inattentive and reluctant to get involved in the activities. Much of the time he watches the clock and stares out of the window.

REFLECT

Fear of failure

Past experience may have taught children to become frightened of failing, of not being able to understand what they have been asked to do or how to do it. Doing well, being always best at everything, never seeming to make mistakes, can become so important that they dare not take a risk.

Children who learn to fear failure may construe themselves as failures. They may have experienced being mocked by other children, when they tried to compete or take part in an activity. They may have failed to win a place in the school of their parents' choice, or be unable to live up to their families' expectations. They may believe they cannot match the achievements of other siblings.

Children who are afraid to take risks can become 'conforming coasters', or teacher pleasers, presenting their work neatly and tidily, doing precisely what is asked of them and never making suggestions that might be rejected by their classmates. They are often heavily reliant on constant reassurance from their teachers. Or, alternatively, they may protect their sense of self-worth through disengaging altogether and pretending they are not interested in doing well.

As a result their learning becomes impoverished. They draw in upon themselves. They miss out on the fun of playing with ideas, of experimenting with unusual or alternative solutions, or learning *through* failure. They lose the thrill of achieving something they had not previously believed they could accomplish.

Failure is part of life, and through failure we can learn how to overcome problems and find solutions. Children need to learn to cope with the challenge of failure and to develop emotional and intellectual resilience, so that they 'learn how learn from their mistakes' and become more successful problem solvers.

REFLECT

Jacob is trouble. He has little respect for school staff and is openly hostile to many of his classmates, who find him arrogant and self-opinionated. Some are even afraid of him. In class he is often in trouble for not paying attention or for distracting others. However, though he rarely contributes in class, his teachers recognise that he is highly intelligent, with a special aptitude for science. Discussions with his mother reveal another side to Jacob. 'Don't be fooled by him', his mother says, 'Jacob is deeply anxious. He is scared of not getting things right, so he puts on this front.' Jacob has internalised unhelpfully high expectations of himself. Arrogance, aggressive challenge and not contributing to class discussion are his way of managing his fear of getting things wrong, or of being able to prove to himself and others that he is clever.

Peer pressure

Peer pressure can be a major cause of underachievement, especially during adolescence. Being accepted as one of the group and being made to feel important by your peers becomes increasingly important in the early years of secondary school. If young people who are deemed to be clever or talented are part of a group where hard work or academic achievement is not valued, or if they have been on the end of disparaging remarks about their intelligence or talent, they may well choose to mask their abilities, and only do what is necessary to get by. 'I work just hard enough to make the teachers think I'm working hard', said Michael. The result can often be wasted years, depression, frustration and disappointment.

High achievement in any field requires effort, determination and perseverance just as much as innate high ability. Teachers cannot create in a child or student the determination to succeed. As Lauren, one of the high-achieving students in the research project, explained, 'It must come from inside.'

However, all schools can combat negative peer pressure by ensuring that the learning opportunities on offer are stimulating, exciting, fun and relevant and by creating an ethos throughout the school that celebrates achievement for all. Individual teachers, through sharing their own passion for their subject, can encourage their students to experience the pleasure and excitement to be found in developing one's own knowledge and skills. Such teachers can stimulate children's belief in themselves and in their unique gifts.

- Are there children in our school/my class, whose ability may be masked by their behaviour? What questions should we/I be asking?
- What evidence do we seek from parents about their children's interests at home and about their possible social and emotional needs?

REFLECT

Good practice in the care and support for the well-being of gifted and talented pupils

The twelve schools that took part in the research project were chosen because of their recognised good practice in meeting the needs of their more able and talented students. The characteristics of their pupil populations varied considerably. Some schools were drawn from Greater London, others served culturally and religiously diverse inner-city communities; whilst others had pupils predominantly from white middle-class or working-class families in market towns or more rural areas.

Each school had developed its own particular character. Each had found ways of tackling underachievement that were relevant to their own communities. They (inter alia) fulfilled the criteria for exemplary practice as set out in the National Quality Standards in Gifted and Talented Education and the NACE Challenge Award:

An ethos of ambition and achievement is agreed and shared by the whole school/college community. Success across a wide range of abilities is celebrated.

The school/college places equal emphasis on high achievement and emotional well-being, underpinned by programmes of support personalised to the needs of potentially able and talented pupils. There are opportunities for pupils to use their gifts to benefit other pupils and the wider community.

(DfES, 2005)

The outstanding feature of all twelve schools was their holistic approach to the education of the children and the care that was taken to ensure that no one, regardless of their abilities, 'slipped through the net'. In these schools, good practice in meeting the personal needs of all pupils and in ensuring their social and emotional well-being was evident through every aspect of school life. It was seen at whole-school level, in the quality of teaching and learning in and beyond classrooms, and in the support for individual pupils.

Good practice at whole-school level

Key features that characterised effective support for the social and emotional well-being of pupils, at whole-school level, included:

- a culture and ethos where everyone, staff, pupils and parents, felt they were valued and had an important part to play;
- carefully designed, detailed and effective systems to assess pupils' performance and progress;
- established procedures for regular reviews at whole-school, subject, class and individual pupil level, to identify needs for development and support;
- early recognition of problems and taking steps to address the concerns;
- systems for 'listening to the voice' of pupils (school forums, school councils, student participation on governing bodies), and taking action on their ideas for school and teaching improvement;
- teachers who were enthusiastic about their work and who were given opportunities to work together on innovative and creative approaches to the curriculum;
- a rich and varied extra-curricular programme to encourage pupils to develop their talents and interests and to engage with others on group activities;
- opportunities (and encouragement) for pupils to make a contribution to school life and to the wider community.

Of particular note in these schools was the importance given to creating an environment in which all the staff felt themselves to be valued as people as well as professionals. Staff in schools share the same fundamental needs proposed by psychologist Abraham Maslow. They need to feel secure in their place within the school community. They need to know that their skills and talents are both recognised and valued. They need opportunities to be creative and to demonstrate that they have an important contribution to make, not only to the pupils in the classes they teach, or with whom they work, but also across the wider community.

The schools in the research project recognised that in order to provide well for pupils they had to provide well for the whole-school community. The welfare of the staff, as well as that of the pupils, was of concern to school management. Staff felt confident in taking 'risks', in pushing the boat out, in putting forward new ideas. Opportunities were provided to design and implement new approaches to teaching and learning both in their own classrooms and more widely in the school. They were allowed to challenge existing practice, even, in some instances, to make significant changes to the National Curriculum. They were able to work in teams and to take the children's educational experiences beyond the school. They had permission to have fun.

Case study: St Marylebone School, London

REFLECT

St Marylebone School (www.stmarylebone.westminster.sch.uk), an 11–18 comprehensive Church of England school for girls, is one of the London Diocesan Board's fifteen secondary schools. Thirteen years ago the school struggled to attract students from the whole ability range. Since then, as a result of the many changes that have taken place, there is now considerable competition for places. Apart from outstandingly thorough procedures for assessing and monitoring students' progress, the school offers an impressive range of extra-curricular opportunities, using the talents within the school staff as well as the rich and varied resources within the community. On any one day in the week there is a choice of between five and ten activities during the lunch-hour and between seven and twenty after school.

However, it is in its approach to teaching and learning within the curriculum, its ability to enthuse staff and pupils and its willingness to look to creative solutions to overcome problems that the school is making its greatest impact on student achievement. 'We have developed a culture of acceptance and openness to reflection on existing practice ... over time we have shifted from a focus on delivering knowledge to that of creating learning' (Deputy Headteacher).

Some years ago, having identified that many of the students were 'treading water' throughout their first year in school, the staff designed a totally new approach to the curriculum. A shortened Key Stage 3 programme was introduced. In effect, this meant covering the whole Key Stage 3 curriculum in Years 7 and 8, and freeing up Year 9 for the introduction of new experiences and innovative, more group- and project-based methods of working. The changes have resulted in tighter, more efficient and dynamic teaching in Years 7 and 8, and opportunities for students to engage in research, marketing and production across a wide range of activities in Year 9. The focus has been on the pupils working collaboratively, and in their working towards delivering an identifiable outcome, be that a performance, or a new product. New relationships have been developed with the local community and with specialist colleges and institutions. These have broadened the opportunities for all pupils and provided able and talented pupils with access to specialist facilities not often available within a school.

A further driving force has been the development of a programme of performing arts across the curriculum, the writing of which involved every teacher in the school. The impact of the school's innovative approaches on the quality of pupils' experience of school has been remarkable. Student motivation is sky high. 'The drama teachers are amazing', said one Year 9 student, who had previously been a reluctant school attender. 'Every year we are able to take part in musicals and plays and we get to work with real drama students from college. I just love coming to school.'

REFLECT

- Do all staff in school feel valued? Are their skills and contributions given due recognition? How do we know? What more could we do?

Good practice at classroom level

The influence of life in the classroom on children's social and emotional well-being is enormous. Children who enjoy their learning experiences become happy and enthusiastic about their work. Alternatively, if they feel they are not valued by their teacher, or fear the reaction of their peers to anything they say or do, they will quickly shut off and take action to protect their vulnerability. There is nothing so painful or alienating than being in a group in which you are not welcome.

The defining characteristic of the work in departments and classrooms in the research project schools, apart from the quality of teaching and learning, was the care and attention given to individual pupils. Teachers were fully aware of the importance of:

- providing a safe, caring, supportive environment in which pupils were respected and where they were taught by example to respect one another (one school was successfully using the Philosophy for Children pro- gramme to support this aim);
- raising and maintaining pupils' expectations of themselves, through both praising their efforts and encouraging them to raise their sights even further;
- fostering creative problem-solving and independent thinking to support the development of the pupils' unique identity and develop their 'resilience' (two schools were using the TASC Problem-Solving Framework as the basis for developing personalised learning);
- conducting research into the possible causes of suspected under- achievement in groups of pupils or in any one individual;
- being willing to be flexible and, if necessary, to reorganise schedules of work or homework demands, according to the needs of particular groups of students or individuals;
- taking risks themselves and using techniques, such as those used in Drama, to raise the emotional level of pupils' responses and enable them to give voice to their ideas and feelings.

Senior managers monitored and responded to classroom practice where improvement or further developments were needed, or where staff needed more support or training.

Case study: Lowes Wong Junior, Southwell

Lowes Wong Anglican Methodist School (www.loweswong-jun.notts.sch.uk) is a large junior school in a busy market town. It serves a mixed, but relatively prosperous catchment area. It is a high-achieving school with a long-standing reputation for high expectations and high achievements across the board. It is also a highly inclusive school and caters effectively for a number of children with very significant special needs.

Teaching and learning throughout the school is characterised by the use of ICT, music, multimedia materials and experiential approaches. Drama and role play are used as everyday techniques in the classroom, as a starting point for discussions and as the basis for children's written work. Staff have found that the physical act of children being up on their feet, of their having to plan with others and get into role releases their energy and encourages the more reticent to express themselves more freely. Drama also acts as an excellent stimulus for language and vocabulary development. It has proven particularly successful in

REFLECT

motivating reluctant writers. Across the school, teachers and learning support staff are encouraged to make learning fun.

Staff know their children well. They are careful to vary the amount of support they give to different children, reducing the information or directions (the teaching scaffolding) they provide for tasks, where this gets in the way of children finding their own solutions.

Respect and care for others is a hallmark of relationships across the school. Pupils are encouraged to act as peer mentors, helping other children in class who are struggling with their work or behaviour. They are invited to assist teachers in planning lessons, designing materials for younger pupils, or sharing their particular talents for the benefit of others. This might include performing in assemblies or leading an activity in school. Pupils are involved throughout the year in designing and running fund-raising activities for charitable causes in this country and abroad.

The headteacher personally monitors the welfare of every child. Where children appear not to be doing as well as they might, or a specific problem is identified, she and the classteacher carefully examine all likely causes. They look for ways to rekindle the children's interest and motivation through personalising the work they are given, or through finding them a special role. Where necessary, significant adjustments are made to arrangements for an individual child.

Good practice in supporting individual pupils

There is no one best way to support children. Children are individuals and their personal history and circumstances may lead to particular ways of coping in school. Therefore certain strategies may be more successful than others in motivating a particular child to succeed. What works for one child may not work for another.

However, the project schools endorsed the following strategies as being particularly effective. They have also been found to be effective in many other schools as well. In the section below they have been grouped according to Belle Wallace's 'typologies' (see Chapter 1).

Children who are working well within their capabilities (coasting or playing safe)

These children may be helped by being:

- challenged through needing to produce an 'end task', such as making a presentation, taking part in a performance, producing a report;

- encouraged to join activities in areas which are not their first choice;
- allowed to take a more creative or different approach to tasks set;
- introduced to a competitive element in tasks set (if they enjoy or are willing to accept challenge);
- asked to act as leaders, peer tutors, coaches or subject specialists where they can share their skills with others.

Anna is considered to be a good all-rounder. She has always been recognised as being bright, but she never likes to put herself forward in any way. Her work is neat and tidy and her homework is always given in on time. She rarely volunteers ideas in class discussion, or asks for help. She is thought to be generally 'doing fine'. But Anna is not really doing fine. She is selling herself short. Anna needs encouragement to break free from the restrictions she is putting on herself. Whilst she needs to be praised for what she does, she also needs to be encouraged to believe she can do so much more. Anna is helped to take a more active role in class by joining a group to produce a campaign for healthy living and by being given a specific role. She finds her artistic skills and the ideas she comes up with are appreciated by the rest of the group. Once she saw how successful the end product was and how much she had enjoyed taking part, she became much more enthusiastic about other aspect of work in class.

REFLECT

Children who find it difficult to concentrate, to organise their work, to persevere or to see a task through (impatient inattentives or butterfly learners)

These children may be helped by:

- being given real tasks with deadlines and an end task (either as an individual, or which requires group contributions to complete);
- working in a group in order to benefit from different learning approaches;
- being challenged by a tailor-made task linked to a personal interest;
- receiving specific guidance on how to organise their work more effectively, with follow-up support.

REFLECT

Rachel hates writing anything down. She is far happier talking to her peers and to her teachers. She is always ready to answer questions and to share her ideas, but she switches off the moment she is asked to record her work. Following an exciting Drama day where the class had re-enacted the Great Fire of London, the pupils are asked to record the events they had dramatised. Rachel settles down glumly to work, showing little enthusiasm. When asked what she had learned during the day, she demonstrates total recall, but says she can't see any point in recording what she already knows. It is so boring. The teacher quickly reframes the task, asking Rachel to build a story around a modern-day equivalent, describing a fire that might have happened in the local town: how it came about, how it was dealt with, illustrating the differences between what might happen now and the events of the Fire of London. Rachel is enthused.

It is important for Rachel to see a purpose for her writing and to use her skill with language more imaginatively. She requires a personalised challenge but it is also important that she should be engaged on work that is linked to what her classmates are doing and that she should not be singled out to be different.

Children who have lost interest in their work and life in school (apathetic non-engagers, mental absentees)

These children may be re-engaged through:

- identifying the cause of their disengagement (which may not be obvious);
- needing to produce an 'end' result which addresses a real-life issue or a real problem that needs to be solved (in school or in the community), where the individual pupil or the group can set their own tasks;
- using the 'All pupils Must, some pupils Should and certain pupils Could' structure for class assignments. The 'Could' task can provide additional challenge and interest for a particular pupil;
- using drama to reduce inhibitions and provide the ideas and language pupils need and to raise emotional level of responses;
- engaging pupils as peer mentors.

David, whom we met earlier, has shut off from school as he had finds it so boring; he needs more colour and fun in his experiences in school in order to kindle his energy and talents. The breakthrough with David comes when he is encouraged to audition for the school musical. He takes a lead role and makes it his own, at times ad-libbing wildly but successfully and injecting imagination and humour into his performance. He is the star. Once his interest in taking part had been revived it becomes possible to talk him through the impact of his behaviour on others and the need to learn to live as a member of society, earning respect through one's contribution to the life of the community.

Another pupil, Joanne longs to learn the piano but has not qualified for free tuition, so lost interest in practising the flute. She also becomes depressed and her other work begins to suffer. Once it is known how much she had wanted to learn to play the piano and how disappointed she is, a teacher in the school volunteers to teach her at lunchtime and becomes her learning mentor.

Children who fear failure (risk avoiders, safe players)

These children may learn to become more confident through:

- being encouraged to become lead learners and take responsibility for communicating with others;
- being encouraged to join creative clubs, to develop resilience;
- using drama to reduce inhibitions and provide ideas and language they need, raising emotional level of responses;
- selectively reducing the information and direction (teaching scaffolding) that gets in the way of them finding their own way to solve problems/find solutions;
- being given problem-solving opportunities for which there are no clear or 'right' answers;
- collaborative learning, working in a group with others on interesting problems that need creative solutions.

Jacob, whom we met earlier, needs teachers who can understand his behaviour and recognise his potential. He also needs opportunities to work from time to time with his intellectual peers on projects or tasks that he can see as having real value. A research team approach, as described in Chapter 5 on research communities, is ideal for Jacob.

Children who have opted out and become antagonistic to work and school life (disaffected disengaged)

These children may be helped through:

- teachers searching out the root cause of the problem, not jumping quickly to conclusions;
- being encouraged to devise their own learning, using the TASC approach, for example;
- behaviour clinics and school counsellors;
- being encouraged to use their talents for the benefit of others, to give master classes, perform in assemblies, assist specialist teachers, etc.;
- pairing them with a peer mentor.

Stephen has opted out. He seems to live in a world of his own and is never where he should be. He is the bane of his teachers as, when he chooses to participate in class, he constantly challenges what the teacher is saying, being sure to correct any small mistake he detects in the information or argument. His work is untidy and carelessly done. At home he lays around watching TV or playing games on the computer.

Yet teachers recognise that Stephen is highly intelligent. When he is interested in what is being done in class, he asks the most perceptive questions and his comments show an unusual level of understanding. He offers unusual solutions to problems. Both staff and parents are frustrated by Stephen's lack of interest and the fact that he appears to be going nowhere.

But Stephen is trying to go somewhere. He is just struggling to find a sense of direction. In discussion with a mentor it turns out that he feels he is biding his time in school and can't see how it relates to his ambition to be an airline pilot. 'How do they know what I am thinking when I stare out of the window,' he says angrily. 'I am not doing nothing, I am thinking plenty.'

Young people like Stephen are hard to teach. It is easy to feel exasperated by the apparent waste of skills and talent. Yet the answer must lie in helping them see the link between what they are doing now and what their dream is for the future, as well as finding ways in which they can find some pleasure and fulfilment in their present.

Children who are unable to demonstrate their abilities because of communication, sensory or physical difficulties (multiply exceptional pupils, or masked gifted)

These children require:

- sensitive procedures for identifying and assessing the barriers to learning and well-being;
- teachers who can recognise their potential;
- appropriate learning and pastoral support;
- flexible arrangements for how they are treated and how they approach their work;
- imaginative use of the resources within the class, school and community.

Ryan, a pupil with autistic spectrum disorder, presents quite a challenge to his teacher. His high level of anxiety and his tendency to rages when he becomes confused or frustrated means that it is difficult, at times, to attend to him as well as the rest of the class. When he is upset, there is no point in admonishing him or demanding that he conform to class rules. Yet the teacher is keen not to make him feel excluded.

The way through with Ryan, who has significant communication difficulties, is to allow him to withdraw when he becomes overstressed. He has a special corner in the classroom where he can cover himself with a blanket for as long as he needs. Or he can seek sanctuary in the headteacher's room in a special place reserved for him. 'It is crucial to choose the right teacher for such a child', says the headteacher. 'We need to be flexible and creative in our approach and provide him with escape routes. We also need to involve the whole class in sharing responsibility for helping Ryan. Caring for others is the hallmark of our school.'

See Chapter 3 on multiple exceptionality.

- How effective are our procedures for supporting more able and talented children? How do we know? What could be done better?
- What opportunities are there in our school/in my class for children to share their talents and skills for the benefit of other pupils and the wider community?
- How does our school ensure children's needs and aspirations are known? How are children able to influence school practice?

Individual support and guidance for pupils

Schools can provide learning environments in which all children feel secure and are able to develop their knowledge, skills and talents to the full. Teachers can plan and deliver lessons and courses that are interesting, exciting and challenging, which offer pupils the chance to develop their particular interests and skills.

But children need more than that. They need to know that the school is watching out for them, that they matter as individuals and that their progress and welfare is being closely monitored. They also need opportunities to review their progress on a regular basis with someone who can help them identify areas for improvement, or where they might wish to put in greater effort.

The twelve schools in our sample held regular reviews with all pupils, not just those with special needs or who were on the gifted and talented register. Such reviews were often termly but more often, where a need arose. The purpose and value of such reviews was to enable the school or the teacher to:

- identify any problem relating to school, lessons, home or relationships and look for solutions;
- identify the pupil's own goals/targets and strategies;
- devise a personalised programme to address areas of risk;
- where necessary, alter school, teacher, student expectations;
- modify work demands;
- make changes to work styles where appropriate.

Reviews also served a useful function for pupils in helping them decide where they wished to direct their efforts.

Nasreen is a Year 13 and Fiona is a Year 12 student. Both are recognised as being very able. However, examination of their work during the year and discussions held with both girls at their termly reviews show that they are not achieving at the level of which they are capable. Both have particular abilities in science but they both have difficulty in organising their work and their time. Homework assignments are handed in late, or not done at all.

Having had other students in the past with similar characteristics, the head of science decides to get these girls to support each other. Nasreen is asked to be Fiona's tutor, to teach her parts of her course work. This means that Nasreen has to prepare for these sessions at home, and in having to explain concepts to another person, she learns how to organise her own thoughts more effectively. She is also asked to set Fiona targets and homework tasks and to meet with her to review her work. Fiona finds it easier to work through topics with another student and is motivated to do her homework when she knows she will be having an individual tutorial. The head of science meets with both girls at lunchtimes to review how things are going and to talk through science topics of their choice. As a result both girls do very well in their A level examinations, achieving A* grades.

Characteristics of effective reviews

Given the importance of 'motivation' as the driving force behind achievement, the essential elements of effective reviews are as shown in Figure 2.2.

• How effective are our current processes for reviewing pupils' progress? How do we know? What training is provided for tutors/mentors in carrying out individual reviews?

REFLECT

Learning or tutoring conversations

A discussion with a child or young person about their work, their progress, or their life in school can be thought of as a 'learning conversation'. However, to be truly effective in helping someone plan what they can do to improve or change what they are doing, such conversations need a framework.

When reviewing progress with pupils, it is all too easy to slip into a 'telling' mode where we tell them what we think about how they are doing and then 'tell' them again what they should do to make any changes or improvements.

And yet, 'telling' is probably the most ineffective way of helping someone. Giving advice, unless it has been specifically requested and fits into the other person's existing plans, is scarcely more useful. There may be many hidden factors or unexplained motives holding that person back from making an

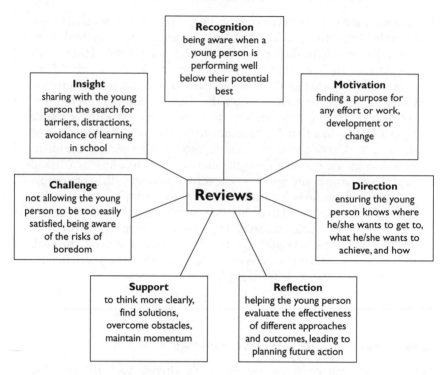

Figure 2.2 Characteristics of effective reviews

effort to improve. Unless we remove these 'barriers' to progress, we are unlikely to be able to offer them genuine help.

Young people are now very familiar with setting objectives for their work. In fact, many students who underachieve (and even some who are successful achievers) become bored with the process and find it an empty exercise. This can be because the targets for improvement are often chosen by others, rather than the young people themselves. Or, too little regard is given to identifying the variety of ways/strategies that might be used to tackle a problem. Similarly, all too often, not enough attention is given to discussing the evidence the young person believes will demonstrate that he or she has succeeded.

We know, from our own experience, that we must first recognise there is a *need* for change or improvement and then *want* that change to occur. We also recognise that we will be more likely to make the effort if we can find ways of making that change happen that are realistic and acceptable to our personal way of working. Only then are we likely to take responsibility for what we learn or achieve. Only then does our learning become 'personalised', and progress or change is likely to occur.

Cathy, who is struggling, resents being told what to do. She finds mentoring unhelpful, as she doesn't like what she interprets as 'intrusive questioning'. She wrestles with achieving standards in her work that satisfy her, but has difficulty in finding a purpose for her work. She also has problems in completing homework to meet teachers' deadlines and so sometimes decides not to bother at all. Cathy clearly needs a different approach to help her overcome her difficulties.

Deborah, on the other hand, whilst having many characteristics of a disaffected, disengaged student, believes that she needs to sort out her problem of underachievement herself. Whereas she recognises she is more likely to succeed in raising the standards of her work by relying on her own resources, she vacillates between blaming herself and blaming staff. She needs help to sort herself out but doesn't know how to ask for it and fears being 'lectured at', which, as she says, would only make her more resentful.

So, if underachieving young people are to become motivated to make greater efforts in their studies, or to try to change some aspect of their behaviour or relationships, they need an approach that explores with greater sensitivity the issues that prevent them succeeding and that helps them identify a goal that is meaningful to them. This may require more time for considering a wider range of strategies for achieving their goals than they normally would use. As has been suggested above, they also need to be given the opportunity to decide on the nature of the evidence that will demonstrate to themselves (and others) that they have been successful.

Structures and strategies to support learning conversations have been devised by a number of educationalists and psychologists working with young people to help them become more motivated, more effective learners.

Salmon Lines, Laddering and *Self-Organised Learning* are three useful approaches. The strategies have also been found effective in bringing about change in a variety of settings at home and abroad: in schools, sports and industry. These approaches, which can be used in conjunction with one another, provide a structure for personalised and constructive 'learning' or 'tutoring' conversations. They also have application for personal and professional development for individuals and organisations.

The strategies used in learning conversations help people to identify a rationale or purpose for what they will be doing, as well as the means of achieving their aims. Through regular reviewing of what is going well, devising more creative and personalised solutions and identifying where difficulties have arisen, people become more effective learners at home, school and work.

Clearly, these techniques are particularly useful in the context of schools in helping students think more clearly about their skills and talents and in encouraging them to constantly evaluate and revise how they manage their work, their lives and their relationships. The strategies also, most usefully, control the potential 'telling' aspect of discussions between a teacher/tutor and student. As such, they draw upon key elements of counselling, coaching and reflective planning.

Salmon Lines

Salmon Lines (Salmon, 1988) employ rating scales to determine how students judge their current performance (in a subject, skill, behaviour, relationship) and what they think could be done to make some adjustment or progress towards achieving a high level of success in their own terms. The process is described below.

Step one: Students are asked to identify some aspect of their work or behaviour that may need improving. They then rate their current situation by placing themselves along a line of 1 to 7 (1 being someone who performs very poorly and 7 being someone who is a star). Alternatively, the student can put words representing opposites at each end of the continuum. For instance: sad and happy, unsuccessful and successful, uncooperative and cooperative, bad teacher and good teacher. The student writes the date just above the score chosen to indicate their current self-rating.

Step two: The teacher/tutor/mentor then takes the student through a detailed set of questions:

- Why have you given yourself that score?
- What is it about your behaviour or your feelings that places you on the score you have currently given yourself?
- What can you do now that you could not do before?

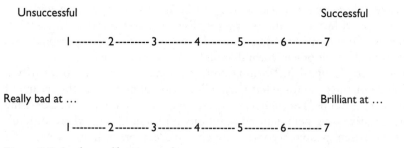

Figure 2.3 Student self-rating scales

- What would the performance/behaviour/ feelings be of someone with the lowest score?
- What does performance, behaviour, skill or state of mind of someone with the highest score look like? What can such a person do that, as yet, you cannot do?

The tutor/mentor writes brief notes on the rating record about what characterises the student's own score and that of the star performer.

Step three: The tutor/mentor invites the student to suggest what s/he needs to be able to do or to change to move up the scale ONE place. Specific behaviours are listed (i.e., achieve a B grade in the mock exam, complete French homework on time, contribute an original idea for the class project, offer to help X in playtime, etc.). If the student cannot provide any suggestions or says 'I'm hopeless at this, I can't get any better', then the tutor invites them to think back a year and asks, 'What can you do now that you could not do then?' Most people will be able to think of something, and this can be used to demonstrate they can make progress in this skill or subject.

Step four: The tutor/mentor discusses what the student now plans to do, what help is needed, how the student will make a start. The decisions are recorded in note form.

Step five: At an agreed time, the tutor/mentor and student meet again to review progress. The student is asked to give her/himself a new rating and asked to explain what their performance now looks like, what has changed and why. A date is recorded for the new score. Again, a detailed exploration takes place. Using, as far as possible, 'open type' questioning, the tutor asks the student to provide specific evidence of how things have changed (if they have) and if not, why they think that this was so. For instance:

- What helped you, or got in your way?
- What did you do then?
- How useful was this?
- How did you feel?
- Why do you think that happened?
- Is there anything you might have done differently?

Step six: If the student wishes to continue to work on improving the same skill, subject or behaviour, the discussion reverts to Step 3. A new discussion takes place on what needs to be done to move up a further point on the scale and how that will be achieved.

The student keeps the Salmon Line Record as evidence of their personal progress towards their goal and the changes achieved over time.

Laddering

Laddering is based on a similar process to Salmon Lines, though this time the student's progress is charted on a vertical, or rising axis and more attention is given to what is the student's underlying purpose for learning or an ultimate goal.

In laddering, the tutoring conversation develops either from a base-line up, or from the identification of a goal or dream, back down to where the student is now.

Laddering, base-line up

The tutor discusses what changes or improvements to their work or behaviour the student wishes to make.

Figure 2.4 Laddering

Working upwards through a series of progressive 'why' questions, the tutor and student explore together why such changes are important to the student. The aim is to identify (where this is not yet clear) something that will act as an important motivator for the student.

Example conversation

What do you want to work on?	Practising the flute more regularly.
Why is that important to you?	I would make more progress.
Why is that important, what difference would it make?	Play more interesting pieces.
How would that make you feel?	Great, I would enjoy playing.
What do you think this will lead to?	Being picked for school orchestra.
What would that mean to you?	My family would be so proud.
Why is that important?	I'd feel I had been a success.
What might be a next step?	Play for the county orchestra.
How important is that for you?	My dream is to get into music school.

Each 'step' is recorded on the ladder.

The discussion then reverts to an examination of the first need: what the student needs to do now about tackling the issue of flute practice (*What's the problem at the moment? What's getting in the way? What might be the ways around this? What incentives could be built in to keep her motivated?*). As time goes by, they can review what has happened and to what extent the student's aims are being fulfilled, and if not, why not.

For many young people, putting an effort into developing skills, for skills' sake alone, seems fairly pointless and boring. But they may be prepared to keep with it if they can be enabled to identify a purpose or a 'dream' and work towards getting somewhere near that dream. For instance, playing football at Wembley, winning Wimbledon, becoming a famous playwright or scientist or singer, being a foreign correspondent, etc.). For this young person, a prime motivator (joining an orchestra) is a means to becoming a success and making her family proud of her. By identifying what is a key motivator in this girl's life, she could be helped to find another source of success and recognition, if the interest in playing the flute does not last.

Laddering, goal first

The tutor helps the student identify a key problem in their work or behaviour. They then look to the much longer term and explore together what the student hopes for the future.

Example conversation

Issue to be worked on: poor grades in maths

How do you see your life in x years' time?	Making lots of money.
What would be your dream job?	Becoming an airline pilot.
Why is that, what would that mean to you?	Travel, exciting life-style.
How do think you will achieve this?	(Discussion of ways forward.)

The long-term goal is placed at the top of the ladder.

(Note: Even though the student's current performance and grades may not appear to suggest this is a realistic goal, the 'dream' must be treated with respect. Whether or not the student is likely to achieve it in the future is not important at this stage. The 'dream' will act as the rationale, or motivator, for the student's efforts to improve his/her existing skills.)

The tutor and student then discuss what they need to do in order to achieve that goal, taking steps down the ladder until they get to the immediate present and what needs to be done right now.

Some examples of laddering-back questions include:

- What skills/qualifications do you think you need?
- What would you have to do to get those skills and qualifications?
- What would you have to be good at?
- What are you good at now?
- What is most likely to hold you back?
- What would you like to get better at?
- How might you improve on what you are doing now?
- What help will you need and who could be most useful to you?

Through such a conversation the student establishes a clearer idea of the path towards the goal and can begin to plan each step up the ladder.

Self-Organised Learning

Self-Organised Learning (SOL) as an approach to learning was developed by Professor Thomas, Director of the Centre for the Study of Human Potential, Brunel University, and Sheila Harri-Augstein, Senior Lecturer in Education, University of Loughborough. The theoretical basis draws on the theoretical work of Rogers' Child Centred Learning, Kelly's Personal Construct Psychology and Buzan's concepts of 'mind mapping'. Kelly was a psychologist, as was Rogers; their work was especially adaptable to education and schools, as well as to working with young people and adults.

The process is similar to many other well-known strategies for developing thinking and planning skills. However, the particular framework for the conversations and the terminology ensure that all the important stages in the process are adequately covered.

SOL provides a clear framework for discussions between two people, where one, the Learner, wants (or needs) to improve some aspect of their work, behaviour or relationships and another, the Tutor, Mentor or Coach, helps them to formulate a plan of action. 'Target-setting' is the term commonly used in schools to describe such activities. But SOL is much more than this. It ensures the young person's ownership of the process and goes much deeper into the factors that may keep them motivated. It also extends their thinking about how to approach the learning task and encourages them to learn from experience.

There are four essential phases to such 'learning conversations': Purpose, Strategy, Outcome and Review (PSOR) as demonstrated in Figure 2.5.

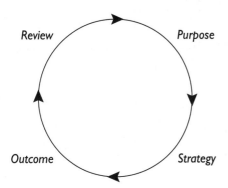

Figure 2.5 The learning conversation

Purpose conversation

Establishing a purpose for whatever the student will attempt to do is paramount. Time must be given to exploring what *the learner* sees as the problem, or to identifying the aspect of their work or life they need or want to improve.

The tutor and young person then discuss what the latter is going to do, why, the purpose for it and how this will improve their work or their life in school or at home. Using the 'base-line up' laddering approach can help set the goal. Salmon Lines may also help the young person identify particular skills/behaviours they may want to work on.

Purposes can be either broad and long term (e.g., become more self-assertive, achieve an A grade in GCSE maths), or specific (make my work neater, get picked for the football team, get my History homework in on time). The purpose is recorded under the Purpose column on the SOL Record Sheet (see Figure 2.6).

Name _____ School _____

Use this sheet to plan what you will try to change and improve, how you will do this and what help you need.

PURPOSE What I will try to do	STRATEGY How I will try to make it work/what help I will need	OUTCOME Evidence that I have succeeded
1. Date		
2. Date		
3. Date		

Figure 2.6 Self-Organised Learning Planning Sheet

Strategy conversation

This conversation is critical in identifying strategies for achieving the learner's goal. We all have our own, often well-established, ways of doing things, but these may not necessarily be the most effective strategies for the task in hand. Children and young people often need help in broadening their ideas and strategies; otherwise they can become mono-strategy learners or responders. 'I always do it this way . . . that's the only way I can think of' they say. If or when their favoured strategy fails, they are likely to give up and say the task itself is hopeless (or, more worryingly, that they themselves are hopeless).

The tutor's task during the 'strategy' discussion is to encourage 'flexible thinking', through identifying as long a list of potential strategies as possible, and to discuss what might be the benefits, drawbacks and consequences for each one that is suggested. For example:

- What could you do to make your work neater?
- How would you set about that?
- How do you think that would help?
- Who/what might help you?
- How would you set about getting that help?
- How might that person respond if you asked them in that way?
- Would that be the only way you could do it?
- Is there anyone else, or anywhere else you could go to?

Having considered a wide range of strategies and their possible consequences, the learner selects one they will try first and records this under the 'How' column of the record sheet.

Outcome conversation

Evidence of achieving goals or targets in school is too often based on outcomes that the young person may not necessarily think are most important. It is therefore essential to identify what the learner believes will indicate they have been successful, or are making progress. It is also important to recognise that goals or outcomes may have both subjective as well as objective components. For instance, the criteria may not only be 'to achieve better grades in science', but also 'to become less anxious and tense before and during the exams'.

Outcomes may be directly related to what the young people have been working on (improving their handwriting, etc.) but may also be something not obviously related but nevertheless very important to them; for instance, 'My parents will be proud of me.' For a young person to feel they are making progress and achieving their aims, it must be the evidence they wish themselves to see or experience that is recorded.

Questions the tutor might ask at this stage include:

- How long do you think this will take?
- When do you expect/hope to see any change?
- How will you know that you have succeeded, improved, made progress?
- What will show you that this is so?
- What will you expect to have happened? How will you feel then? Why is that important?

The expected outcomes are recorded under the 'Outcome' column of the record sheet.

Review conversation

At an agreed time, learner and tutor meet to review what has happened.
At this stage they talk about the original need and purpose:

- Was this a realistic aim for you?
- Did it turn out to be a useful thing to work on?

They then review the usefulness of strategies used:

- Was the strategy you used successful? If not, why not?
- Did you try another way? Was that approach any better?
- Who helped you and how?
- Could you have done anything differently?

Finally, they look at the outcomes:

- Was the time-scale realistic? Did you give yourself enough time, too much time?
- What has changed? How do you know? How do you feel?
- Did anything else happen as a result of you working on this target?

The conclusion could be a discussion about what the young person wants to do next. This might be to continue working on the same target but aiming for a higher level, or employing a new strategy, or a change to the expected outcome. Or, it might be to change direction and work on something else, using a new PSOR plan?

Life conversation

At any time during the Purpose, Strategy, Outcome conversations it may become apparent that the learner's progress towards their initial goal is being obstructed by some other factors in their lives (a difficulty at home, in a relationship with peers or staff, or with access to materials or support). Where this happens it may be necessary to suspend the original plan and move into another loop, the 'life conversation'. The same process of Purpose, Strategy, Outcome, Review is then followed (What do you need to do? How could you do this? What will be the result?), before returning, where relevant, to the original objective in the learning conversation.

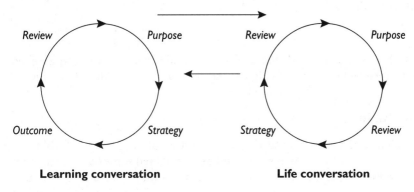

Learning conversation   **Life conversation**

Figure 2.7 Tutoring conversations

Using SOL conversations

The process outlined above may appear onerous and time consuming. However, it can be used in many ways, from a reasonably brief conversation (What are you trying to do? How are you going to do it? What do expect it to look like? How will you know if you have done what you wanted?), to in-depth interviews, which more fully explore the young person's needs and wants and plans.

It can be also used with very young children as part of normal discussions about their work, as well as with young people and adults planning more complex tasks. The most important aspect of the conversations is the *embedding* of a thinking, planning and review process into learners' everyday ways of working, so that they become skilled at solving problems and planning their work for themselves. This way they become more effective and efficient learners and performers.

SOL conversations are especially useful for discussions with very able and talented young people who, as we have discussed, may previously not have faced difficulties in their learning and may have found success came too easily. In other words, they may not have learnt how to learn.

Mark has sailed through school, taken his GCSEs and A levels early, achieving a raft of A grades. He arrives at university expecting to be able to do the same, only to find he is unable to cope with the higher level of demand on his mathematics course. He does not really know how to organise his studies. He has never developed the self-discipline of hard work and effort. His whole sense of self is shaken and he drifts out of education. As he later admits 'someone who is motivated and knows how to set about their work in an organised way and is prepared to work really hard, irrespective of their IQ, is more likely to be successful than the "brilliant" individual without a sense of direction'.

Mark's experience and that of others like him could have been avoided had he received the kind of help offered through Self-Organised Learning.

Conclusion

This chapter has considered the social and emotional needs of able and talented children and young people. It has highlighted some of the issues that these young people face, both at home and in school, and described examples of good practice observed in the twelve research project schools. Different ways of engaging with young people about their work have been outlined.

The theme running throughout the chapter has been the importance of establishing an ethos throughout the school of care and concern for the individual, where the needs and aspirations of children and staff are known, where their talents and creativity are fostered and where everyone is able to make a valued contribution to the whole community.

Senior managers and staff may wish to make use of the 'Points for Reflection', to reflect on practice in their own school.

- How effective are our procedures for supporting gifted and talented children? How do we know? What do we think could be done better?
- Are there children in our school/in my class, whose ability may be masked by their behaviour? What questions should we/I be asking?
- What evidence do we seek from parents about their children's interests at home and about their possible social and emotional needs?
- What opportunities are there in our school/in my class for children to share their talents and skills for the benefit of other pupils and the wider community?
- How does our school ensure children's needs and aspirations are known? How are children able to influence life in school?

- Do all staff in school feel valued and are their skills and contributions given due recognition? How do we know? What more could we do?
- How effective are our current processes for reviewing pupils' progress? How do we know? What training is provided for tutors/mentors in carrying out individual reviews?

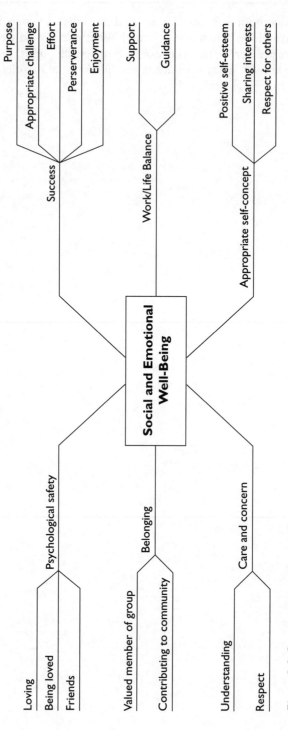

Figure 2.8 Summary concept map 2

References and further reading

Bannister, D. and Fransella, F. (1986) *Inquiring Man: The Psychology of Personal Constructs*. London: Penguin.

Buscemi, M. Poem: *The Average Child*. http/:holyjoe.net/poetry/buscemi.htm.

Buzan, T. (1993) *Use Your Head*. London: BBC Publications.

DfES (2005) *National Quality Standards in Gifted and Talented Education*. HMSO.

Freeman, J. (1991) *Gifted Children Growing Up*. London: Cassell.

Fisher, R. (1995) *Teaching Children to Think*. Cheltenham: Stanley Thorne Publishers.

Lee Corbin, H. and Denicolo, P. (1998) *Recognising and Supporting Able Children in Primary Schools*. London: David Fulton Publishers.

Leyden, S. and Leyden, G. (2009) 'Children first, a strategy for inclusive education in Nottinghamshire', in Bunch, G. and Valeo, A. (eds) *Inclusive Education: Emergent Solutions*. Toronto: Inclusion Press.

Leyden, S. (2002) *Supporting the Child of Exceptional Ability, At Home and School*. 3rd edition, revised and extended. London: NACE/Fulton Publication.

Lipman, M. *et al.* (1980) *Philosophy in the Classroom*. 2nd edition. Philadephia: Temple University Press

Maslow, A. H. (1954) *Motivation and Personality*. Harper: New York.

Murris, K. (1992) *Teaching Philosophy with Picture Books*. London: Infonet Publications.

Nottinghamshire County Council (1999) *Able Pupils: Providing for Able Pupils and Those with Exceptional Talent*. Nottinghamshire Education Department Publications.

Salmon, P. (1988) *Psychology for Teachers*. London: Hutchinson.

Thomas, L. and Augstein, S. (1991) *Learning Conversations: The Self-organised Learning Way to Personal and Organisational Growth*. London: Routledge and Kegan Paul.

Stopper, M. J. *et al.* (2000) *Meeting the Social and Emotional Needs of Gifted and Talented Children*. London: NACE/David Fulton Publishers.

Wallace, B., Fitton, S., Leyden, S., Montgomery, D., Pomerantz, M. and Winstanley, C. (2007) *Raising the Achievement of Able, Gifted and Talented Pupils within an Inclusive School Framework: Guidelines for Schools to Audit and Extend Existing Best Practice*. Oxford: National Association for Able Children in Education. publications@nace.co.uk.

Wallace, B. *et al.* (2004), *Thinking Skills and Problem Solving: An Inclusive Approach*. London: David Fulton Publications.

Wood, D. (1999) *How Children Think and Learn*. Oxford: Blackwell.

Articles directly available from the author sueleyden@mac.com:

I'm OK, You're OK, Social and Emotional Needs of Children with Exceptional Abilities

Why Not Talk to the Pupils, Raising Standards of Excellence

You and Your Relationships . . . The Teenage Years

Chapter 3

Gifted and talented children with special educational needs

Lifting underachievement in dual and multiple exceptionalities

Diane Montgomery

Introduction

In the gifted education field, dual or double exceptionality (2E) is a term used to describe those learners who are potentially very able or who have a talent (a special gift in a performance or skill area) and in addition to this have a special educational need (SEN) such as dyslexia, or ADHD.

This is made more complex when children may not demonstrate their 'gifts' and the SEN may be hidden or 'masked'. These pupils then underachieve, but their underachievement (UAch) may also go undetected, and they become trebly disadvantaged.

If they come from homes that are disadvantaged in social or cultural terms or are from ethnic minority backgrounds, even British Minority Ethnic (BME) groups, they will suffer compound disadvantages in many schools. Importantly, the staff in the schools in the original research case studies are exceptionally alert and sensitive to the possibility of a five-fold, and hence, almost insuperable complexity of disadvantage.

Recent evidence (DCFS, 2009b) finds that family background is still the major determinant of success. Even now, very few children from 'working-class' homes gain places at the top universities and access to high status jobs, despite being potentially very able.

Dual exceptionality is well known in the SEN field. It is termed co-morbidity and often occurs in dyslexia when the dyslexic may also show symptoms of attention deficit hyperactivity disorder (ADHD), Asperger's syndrome (AS) or dyspraxia (DCD, developmental coordination difficulties).

In all four conditions – dyslexia, ADHD, AS and DCD – there is also a high frequency of co-occurrence of handwriting coordination difficulties making a multiple exceptionality. This factor alone has a powerful effect because so much time in schools is still spent on writing activities. However, the impact of this is too often ignored and the pupil has a 'hidden' difficulty that lowers performance even if the 'giftedness' and the dyslexia are recognised and provision is made.

The hidden difficulty in many potentially able underachievers is an inability, or an unwillingness, to produce written work of a suitable quality to match the perceived potential (Montgomery, 2000, 2003). Hidden beneath this profile are two problems – a handwriting coordination difficulty and a spelling problem. The spelling problems appear to have a more serious effect. They not only slow down the writing speed (Montgomery, 2008) in important examinations leading to lower grades, but also impact upon the organisation and quality of composition at all grade and university levels.

Across the age groups and ability levels, 30 per cent of pupils have difficulties in writing legibly and at an appropriate speed. Many of them experience physical pain from writing and avoid it whenever possible (ibid.). The problems increase as pupils grow older since for many school subjects the amount of writing required increases. Turning to keyboarding does not always overcome the problem since some pupils also have difficulties with this.

Disadvantage and low socio-economic status can handicap expression and social communication and this too contributes to poor writing.

What are the links between UAch and multiple exceptionalities?

The three factors in Figure 3.1 interact with each other to create different patterns of underachievement and exceptionality.

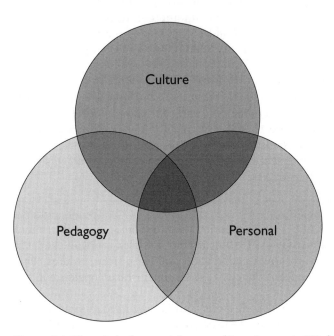

Figure 3.1 The triad of potential areas of impairment in UAch

Alex, a bright boy, is placed in a classroom where the teaching methods are mundane and there is no differentiation or intellectual challenge. He quickly becomes bored and seeks other forms of 'entertainment'. These include annoying other pupils and upsetting the teacher through misbehaviour and clowning. Over time, a reputation for being a behaviour problem develops, and a career in disruption begins which ends in exclusion.

Underachievement is particularly likely to happen when children from disadvantaged backgrounds do not have the language and social skills to divert attention from the misdeeds, or the teacher has poor classroom management skills. A double exceptionality has been *created* in the form of SEBD (social, emotional and behavioural difficulties).

Highly able children in these circumstances will underachieve unless they have the good fortune to meet a mentor, or are rescued from the situation by an understanding teacher.

The personal qualities of Jess, in a similar situation to Alex, mean that she goes to considerable lengths to fit in and conform. In the Early Years it involved helping other children by passing the time hearing them read and helping them write. She became a teacher's aide and teaching assistant.

As the classroom organisation became less flexible in secondary school, she turns to inner mental resources and daydreams the days away. Fortunately she has a home environment that promotes learning and helps to compensate to some degree for the poor schooling. However, with lack of challenge and no failures to learn from, she does not develop the advanced study skills needed to cope with university and dropped out after the first year.

Because of the lack of challenge in both these situations, these children will not learn appropriate study skills to deal with complex work in the later years. Nor will they learn how to cope with, and learn from, failures. This will be further compounded if there is a lack of linguistic competence in the cultural background.

These examples show that 'acting out' and 'acting in' patterns so often seen in SEBD depend very much on the personality of the children. What we do know from research is that both patterns can be turned round by changes

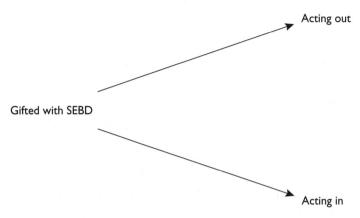

Figure 3.2 Gifted with SEBD

to the teaching methodology and the behaviour management strategies employed by the teacher (Montgomery, 2002). How this is achieved will be outlined in later sections in this chapter.

Dual and multiple exceptionalities exist in the personal area that can create barriers to learning. In addition to the personal qualities that the pupil brings to the situation such as motivation, persistence and personality, there may also be specific learning difficulties (SpLD). In later sections in this chapter, it will be shown how the teaching methods and, in some cases, the curriculum adopted, as well as skilled behaviour management, can alleviate many of the problems and enable the child to achieve at an appropriate level.

What problems arise with regard to dual exceptionality?

Potential 'giftedness' with SEN brings about special problems. Students given provision for their dyslexia, such as remedial teaching and supportive strategies, may be placed in the lowest sets because of their low attainments. This is extremely frustrating for them because then they do not have the stimulation needed to meet or match their high ability. The result is that they can develop behavioural and emotional problems as well and then become a multiple exceptionality case. At each point the SEN can be the focus for intervention and the high ability is overlooked. Moreover, the SEN teachers may not have been trained to understand the needs of the more able.

If the high ability is identified and special provision is made, then the pupil may not perform well because there may be a lack of teaching skill in relation to the SEN. There may also be the problem of needing dual funding to compensate for the dual needs that the education system does not supply. Currently, set funding for one need cannot be allocated to another.

However, when we use inclusive teaching methods, many of these difficulties can be overcome (Montgomery, 2000; Wallace, 2000) and this raises questions about the efficacy of, for example, setting by 'ability'.

Some benefits of mixed ability inclusive teaching

See Box 3.1 for a summary of Hallam's research (2002: 89) on mixed ability teaching.

Box 3.1 Advantages of mixed ability, inclusive class grouping

Mixed ability grouping can:

Provide
- a means of offering equal opportunities
- role models for less able pupils
- a sense of continuity for primary pupils when they transfer to secondary school
- ways of addressing the negative social consequences of structured ability grouping by encouraging cooperative behaviour and social integration.

Promote
- good relations between pupils
- enhanced pupil/teacher interactions.

Enable
- some of the competition engendered by structured grouping to be reduced
- pupils to work at their own pace.

Encourage
- teachers to acknowledge that the pupils in their class are not a homogeneous group
- teachers to identify pupil needs and match learning tasks to them.

However, Hallam warns that to engage in successful mixed ability or inclusive teaching, the teachers need to be highly skilled and appropriately trained and to have at their disposal a wide range of differentiated resources to match to their pupils' needs.

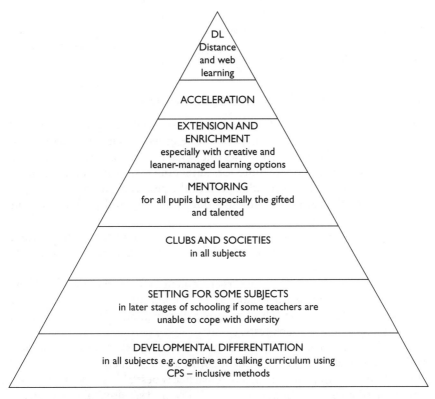

Figure 3.3 The seven provision options that the case-study schools offer for
lifting underachievement

Inclusive teaching groups are a significant feature in the schools in the
original case-study research. There is systematic and extensive continuing
professional development (CPD) for all the staff, including teaching assistants
and governors. In several schools, parents can also join special classes to learn
how to help their children whilst developing their own skills.

Auditing general provision

The levels of provision illustrated in Figure 3.3 can be used as a checklist in
each curriculum area and in each class to identify if a full range of provision
opportunities are on offer. The audit is needed since teachers can think that
because learners have been set by ability, or the school accelerates the 'gifted',
that the 'problem' is solved. There needs to be flexibility in the kinds of
provision on offer and in the methods of grouping learners to suit different
purposes.

For example, on occasions, learners can be formed into vertical age groups, which can bring many benefits. Vertical grouping has been widely used and is a successful strategy adopted by small rural schools. An example of vertical grouping is used in one of the case-study schools for master classes in writing. Most school clubs work effectively on this principle.

Why develop identification through provision?

Once the provision has been audited, particular strategies can be developed as appropriate for identifying pupils' strengths through provision. The case-study schools that were observed engage in a significant degree of identification through opportunity or 'authentic' assessment because of the range and nature of the curriculum and of the pedagogical approaches they use. Many of the techniques involve pupils leading and problem-solving individually and in groups.

This gives the teachers more time to stand back and observe what is going on. They can see how effective the children's learning is, as well as judging how suitable the resources are.

IQ tests rarely, if ever, tap into learners' potential for learning and problem-solving: the tests 'measure' what has been committed to memory during upbringing and education. This becomes a disadvantage if the G + T register is overly dependent on such tests.

The schools in the case studies use a wide range of identification techniques and tracker packages. But it is through the more challenging and creative curriculum tasks that the well-trained teacher is best able to identify a more able pupil or an underachiever. Teachers' close and sensitive observation can also enable the tasks to be adjusted or developed to meet a particular need, or can direct long-term planning. A number on an IQ test or a pattern on a hypothetical set of test sub-skills cannot do this.

Although most schools put 10 per cent of their pupils on the G + T register in England, many schools also have a 'shadow' register indicating a much wider group of pupils. In Wales, the G + T register includes 20 per cent of pupils, which corresponds with the same percentage on the SEN register. This seems a much more realistic approach; however, even this arrangement echoes the old UK 'grammar school' selective system that failed to identify many of the most gifted and talented pupils.

This organisation of such 'registers' also omits those children who are learning disabled (with SpLD) and whose disabilities depress the IQ scores and the school attainments. Silverman (2004) suggests that when there is such a learning disability, at least 10 IQ points should be added to the overall IQ test results when selecting for special gifted education provision, or for the G + T register. This will still not capture those whose Standardised Attainment Test scores (SATs) are depressed by writing difficulties and may exclude all those with SpLD as already indicated.

As we have become more aware that particular kinds of socio-economic deprivation can lead to disadvantage on certain kinds of achievement, 'value added' statistics have been introduced which indicate pupils' educational growth over a period of time. But even this is an *outcome* measure and does not indicate pupils' growth in a dynamic sense. We need an education system that creates opportunities for pupils to demonstrate their gifts and talents through creative and varied provisional opportunities.

Box 3.2 Broad patterns in identification of double exceptionality – 3 Ds

- *Group 1* (usually identifiable – *discrepant 2E*) have been identified by discrepancies between high scores on or within ability tests and low achievements in SATs.
- *Group 2* (usually the disability masks the abilities – *deficit 2E*) have a specific learning difficulty – the ability goes unidentified in the presence of depressed ability test scores and in SATs.
- *Group 3* (usually not identified – *deceptive 2E*) have ability measures and SATs results that seem to fall within the average but not the highly able range.

It is a good idea for staff to reflect on the broad patterns of double exceptionality and to discuss the strategies the school uses to diagnose the full range of pupil needs.

Identifying barriers to learning in SpLDs

Figure 3.4 provides a map of the main types of different special needs including giftedness and talent. As already noted, standard identification procedures may not, unless carefully scrutinised, reveal that a pupil has a special need or is underachieving. Figure 3.4, together with the stages outlined, can be useful in diagnosing the special needs of some pupils.

In the sections that follow, examples and cases of the SpLD are discussed as well as the extent to which the provision made for them can be inclusive.

In the case-study research schools, each school is attempting to lift the achievement of *all* pupils. Careful, regular reviews of all pupils' needs and progress are in place: the headteacher, the SENCo, the class teacher, the G + T coordinator and the parent/carer (where appropriate) are involved. Understandably, in secondary schools these responsibilities need to be more widely dispersed, but the key is that every pupil should be monitored and their needs well known to a relevant group of staff who can coordinate planning and action.

OTHER	DCD – G Developmental Coordination Difficulties – gross	ASD – AS Autistic Spectrum Difficulties and Asperger Syndrome	D – RS + H Dyslexia Reading, Spelling and Handwriting Difficulties (DCD)
BME Black Minority Ethic	DCD – F Developmental Coordination Difficulties – fine, esp. Handwriting	G + T Gifted and/or Talented	D – RS Dyslexia – Reading and Spelling Difficulties
EAL English as an Addititional Language	VMI Visuomotor Integration Difficulties	SEBD Social, Emotional and Behavioural Difficulties	D – S Dyslexia – Spelling only Difficulties, dysorthographia
SES Socio-Economic Status/Class	ADHD/ADD Attention Deficit Hyperactivity Disorder	SLI – R/E Specific Language Impairment – Receptive and/or Expressive	SLCN Speech, Language and Communication Needs

Name of particular pupil _____

Year? _____

Male or Female? _____

Simply shade in any boxes that you think might represent this pupil

Figure 3.4 Double exceptionality – key to main areas

The common theme that is found in twice or thrice exceptional groups is that the majority of these gifted and talented pupils are very good orally, but are poor at writing ideas down at more than an average or even more limited level (Wallace, 2000; Montgomery, 2000). It is essential that this aspect is addressed in any provision offered, since it may represent the hidden difficulty.

Patterns of Special Educational Needs (SEN) and 2E: Gifted Learning Disabled (GiLD)

There are six main types of difficulty that children with SEN might show, and some will have complex learning difficulties involving several conditions.

In the following section the core features of the specific difficulty are identified so that interventions can be appropriately targeted.

The special educational needs' categories in the UK are:

- GLD – General or global learning difficulties – 'slower' learners. Their main difficulties lie in the intellectual area, specifically with limitations in

memory, language and thinking abilities areas. Giftedness can occur in all the categories of SEN except in those with general learning difficulties. Even so pupils with GLD may also be identified with specific talents.

- SpLD – Specific learning difficulties (learning disabilities, e.g. dyslexia, DCD; ADHD/ADD and SLI (see below). These pupils have difficulties in the area of literacy skills in dyslexia; in attention and behaviour in ADHD; in motor coordination and visuo-motor skills in DCD; and disorders in the language areas in SLI.

- PSM – Physical, sensory (hearing and visual impairments) and medical difficulties. These students are in the smallest numbers compared with the other groups. Potentially gifted students with *physical* difficulties, such as cerebral palsy, and *medical* difficulties, such as spina bifida, multiple sclerosis and epilepsies, need access not only to the buildings but also to an intellectually challenging curriculum suited to their individual level of ability. It should be the least of the barriers they have to overcome. Sensory difficulties are the visual and hearing impairments. Although the measures generally used to aid identification also tend to recognise attainments, they do not identify potential. Further barriers are that teachers may be reluctant to include children with sensory and physical difficulties in their extended projects because they lack experience of working with them. For those with hearing impairment using visual scales of tests and Raven's Progressive Matrices (Raven, 2008) as the marks of the potential can help identification of giftedness. Visually impaired but very able students often say they need to be better than 'gifted' students without disabilities in order to be recognised: they share this in common with 'gifted' girls and socially disadvantaged and minority ethnic groups. When more able students with PSM have their specific needs catered for, their educational needs are much the same as other highly able children, and there is now an array of technology that can help them. Even so, they will need as much support as the other groups because of the degree of underachievement.

- SEBD – Social, emotional and behavioural difficulties. These range widely from mild attention-seeking to disruptive behaviour, and also from anxiety reactions to school phobia and bullying.

- SLCN – Speech, language and communication needs or difficulties. SLI is often included in this group as well as those with ASD language impairments.

- Learning disorders – autistic spectrum disorders (ASD) including Asperger's syndrome (AS); specific language impairment (SLI); and Down's syndrome (DS). Sometimes severe SEBDs are included in this group as conduct disorders.

To avoid the confusion when the groups overlap different categories, it is helpful to regard all the conditions as:

1   On a *continuum* from mild difficulties through moderate to severe and profound.
2   Of a particular nature such as a result of:
    - *Delay* – usually a developmental slowness, but following a normal pattern – for example, in GLD and SLCN. Pupils need a slower but normal developmental programme.
    - *Deficit* – usually hinders development, but may clear up later – for example, dyslexia – but not in all cases – and DCD, ADHD can be remediated by specific programmes to a considerable degree.
    - *Disorder* – does not follow a normal pattern of development or clear up later – for example, SLI, ASD, AS, DS – but can be improved by specific training.
3   Needing early intervention in the preschool years and the early years of schooling for all these types of SEN.

General principles and practices in provision

Provision that enables gifts and talents to develop

A critical element to meet the learning needs of most learners, including the potentially able, is the development of a *cognitive* and a *talking* curriculum. The methods are essentially part of inclusive teaching methods. These are methods that enable learning to be collaborative, constructive and extensively oral, not learning led largely by teacher didactics (Montgomery, 2000, 2009a).

A cognitive curriculum

The UK National curriculum guidelines are stressing the need for a *cognitive* curriculum which includes teaching and learning strategies such as:

- Assessment for Learning (AfL);
- positive developmental cognitive feedback on performance, with self-assessment and peer-assessment as key features;
- challenging and open problem-posing and questioning that encourages reasoning;
- deliberate teaching of thinking skills – for example, The TASC Problem-Solving Approach;
- reflective learning and teaching – for example, Lipman's Philosophy for Children;
- creativity training and experiential opportunities;
- cognitive process strategies or teaching methods (CPS) – for example, using cognitive process and research study skills; problem-based learning including real problem-solving and investigative learning; games,

simulations and role play; experiential learning; collaborative learning and team-building opportunities.

In all the case-study schools, the above approaches have resulted in high levels of pupil motivation, with involvement and long-term commitment to the tasks they have undertaken. Truancy decreased especially with disaffected pupils who remain at school and enjoy these personalised, active and extended learning experiences. The collaborative nature of many of the tasks means that mixed ability groups can easily access the work and all can be included in the same broad topics, working at different levels according to varying abilities (Montgomery, 2000).

Several of the case-study primary schools have found the incorporation of Lipman's (1991) *Teaching Philosophy to Children* a very effective way of stimulating all the pupils to enjoy and engage with school activities and rise to intellectual challenges.

The TASC Problem-Solving Approach (Wallace, 2000) is implemented in several schools as a framework that encourages 'expert' thinking and problem-solving whilst, at the same time, developing learners' ownership of their learning, a range of basic and advanced thinking skills as well as essential research and recording skills.

Accelerated Learning is also used in some schools to promote learning, especially through projects such as CASE (Cognitive Acceleration through Science Education) developed by Shayer and Adey (2002). A key aspect is the reflective discussion that is part of the learning programme. A mathematics acceleration project is operating in one primary school supported by Cambridge University, and a science problem-solving project as well as a technology project are being mentored by local secondary school pupils.

The government has actively encouraged these approaches, building on the successful projects emanating from the *Excellence in Cities* initiative (DfEE, 1999) and funding the systematic training developed for G + T coordinators at Oxford Brookes University and through national and regional conferences and training programmes. At the same time, similar approaches were being developed for Key Stage 3 pupils to develop more effective teaching and learning in foundation subjects (Higgins, 2002), leading forward to the Personalising Learning initiative (DfES, 2004–2009). Ofsted will also be auditing the provision for cognitive stretch and challenge.

A talking curriculum

The UK National Curriculum guidelines and strategy documents emphasise the primary importance of developing listening and speaking skills: a *talking* curriculum is perceived as the essential underpinning of reading and writing skills. Most learners, especially those with double exceptionality, need to talk things through before attempting to write their ideas down. Therefore, we

REFLECT

need to audit the *range* of activities that learners are engaged in to ensure talk can take place.

Expect to find the following strategies: think–pair–share, circle time, role play, collaborative work, peer tutoring, book clubs and so on. Moreover, the current emphasis on developing project work means that pupils can engage in *extended* personalised learning activities that encourage greater depth and breadth of learning.

Children with speech, language and communication difficulties (SLCN)

Dyslexics and those with DCD and SEBD can participate more easily in classrooms where they have the opportunities to take an active role in their own learning and where talk and reflection is valued *more than* the written work. In these classrooms the talk clarifies pupils' ideas and promotes the motivation to commit to paper or screen; and the problem-based nature of the work personalises the intellectual challenge.

Provision to overcome SEBD

SEBD is one of the most common difficulties that can mask high ability and result in underachievement. Bright boys and girls find a lack of intellectual challenge in the school curriculum which causes them to become bored and frustrated. The boredom creates 'dead time' in which to find mischievous ways to occupy them to the annoyance of teachers! As noted earlier, many of them 'act out' their frustration and disaffection, while others 'act in' and become passive and dreamy, losing contact with the school routines. The significance of dead time, lack of cognitive stretch and challenge and its contribution to behaviour problems has been recognised in the Steer Report (DCSF, 2009a). This is the latest report on BESD (behaviour, emotional and social difficulties). The report recommends that schools should take into account their teaching and learning strategies when developing their behaviour policies and individual education support plans.

Gifted entrepreneurs in the Confederation for British Industry (CBI) who had failed in school reported becoming 'school averse' and difficult to manage and were excluded or opted out of school early. Their talents and abilities went unnoticed.

As well as SEBD caused by a lack of cognitive challenge, there is also a significant number of bright pupils who bring problems with them from dysfunctional or disadvantaging environments. This makes them unable to fit easily into school routines and demands.

The following list shows some origins of SEBD in potentially able students:

- 'career giftedness' (Freeman, 1991);
- a boring and mundane curriculum; lack of cognitive challenge;

- overactivity, high energy levels;
- hostility to talent from teachers; fear of high ability by teachers;
- bullying by pupils of 'boffs';
- too much time on computers;
- attention-seeking needs, family driven;
- rigid parenting or schooling;
- lack of self-regulated study and choice;
- sexism, racism, perceived difference;
- subcultural disadvantage, social class;
- age differences and treatment of accelerated learners;
- inappropriate models and mentors;
- coercive educational ethos;
- learning difficulties.

Strategies for dealing with SEBD – classroom management

There has been a great awareness of, and training in, the use of positive strategies for behaviour management in classrooms. Teachers have developed a variety of 'fun' routines that they discuss with the pupils, which include the following:

- *Catch them being good!* The emphasis is placed on spotting, praising and rewarding 'good' behaviour, so that self-esteem is reinforced.
- *Ensure variety of activities!* Classrooms abound with a variety of creative and kinaesthetic activities that allow learners freedom for movement and creative self-expression.
- *Use short visual and verbal signals!* Many classrooms use visual signals such as traffic lights, hand signals and short action songs that pupils enjoy and respond to.
- *Use Assessment for Learning techniques with constructive feedback.*
- *Give opportunities for problem-solving activities.*

There are two important aspects of SEBD provision: to create a positive classroom climate and structure for learning, and to design tasks that induce intrinsic interest and offer personal fulfilment. These reduce misbehaviour.

Specific learning difficulties (SpLD)

Dyslexia origins and provision

DEVELOPMENTAL DYSLEXIA (D – RS)

In 'dyslexia' the ability to learn to both read and spell is seriously depressed however bright the pupil. Too often the diagnosis is based upon lack of progress in reading and intervention is targeted on this. Most of the research suggests that the core problem underlying the dyslexia is lack of phonological awareness. However, I suggest that it is not a *cause* but a *result* of the failure.

The core disability in dyslexia is a failure to develop sound-symbol correspondence. So we must ask, why it is that a highly able child at five years who may have an encyclopaedic knowledge of the galaxy or prehistoric monsters is unable to learn the names and sounds of twenty-six letters of the alphabet?

Even if phonics is systematically taught from the outset, 1 to 2 per cent of children still fail to learn the alphabetic principle. Many dyslexics by about the age of eight years finally make the breakthrough and learn. By this time, however, they are up to three years behind their peers in literacy and cannot catch up without specialist help because the normal literacy teaching is beyond their level and speed.

What we can observe is that once they begin to become literate, their progress does follow a normal, if delayed, pattern but not a disordered one (Montgomery, 1997). We therefore need to target intervention in the Reception Year so the breakthrough comes at the right time.

Early identification of dyslexia in Reception   This can easily be undertaken in the first weeks in school by asking all pupils to write a message or their news in any way they can and then noting which scripts do not incorporate any of the sounds taught and which ones indicate coordination difficulties or delays.

The ratio of boys to girls in the dyslexic category varied in the cohorts in my research, but overall the ratio was 1.2:1 boys to girls (Montgomery, 2008). Recent government-funded research at Hull University has shown that of 1300 pupils failing SATs at seven and eleven years, over 50 per cent on further investigation showed 'dyslexic type' difficulties (i.e., reading and spelling problems). (Fuller details of this research and practice may be found in Montgomery (2007) *Spelling, Handwriting and Dyslexia.*)

Developmental dyscalculia   Although recent research by Butterworth (2006) offers a different interpretation, I have not yet encountered a 'dyscalculic' whose difficulties could not be explained by poor or rushed teaching combined with the dyslexic problems with verbal labelling and phonological codes. These difficulties impair digit span recall (working memory), mental arithmetic and reciting and using multiplication tables especially 7s, 8s and 9s. With insufficient concrete experience and lack of talking through sum stories, these pupils frequently fail to understand estimation or grasp the intricacies of place-value and are lost from there on.

Jack: End of Reception Year

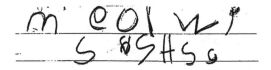

Michael: Year 5

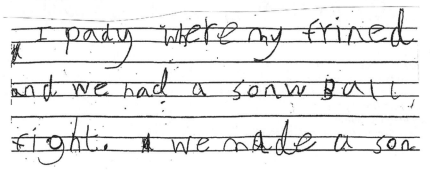

Figure 3.5a Some case examples of dyslexics' written work

DEVELOPMENTAL DYSORTHOGRAPHIA D – S

Dysorthographia is a severe difficulty in learning to spell in the presence of very good or adequate reading ability. It appears common in very able children who often learn to read self-taught, but their spelling is regarded as 'atrocious'. It is also evident in children who are very determined and persistent and go to great lengths to overcome their dyslexia.

With good remedial support, most dyslexics do eventually learn to read but their reading remains slow and their spelling is poor.

Identifying spelling problems is easy but the misspellings are often thought to be 'bizarre'. This is not the case: most errors are based on a poor and incomplete grasp of phonics together with some 'look and say' errors (Montgomery, 2008).

In my researches, the very bright dyslexics made up 10 per cent of the dyslexic groups (IQ 130 points and above) and 34 per cent of this group of 300 dyslexics had at least one IQ scale of 120 points and above. (Now add ten points to their scores as suggested by Silverman to reflect their real ability.)

Jake: Year 6

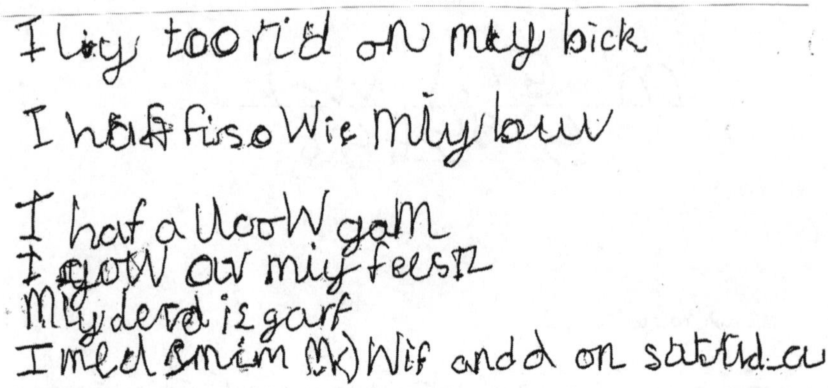

'I like to ride on my bike
I have fights with my brother
I have an old fashioned game (computer)
I go over (to) my friends
My friend is Gareth.
I went swimming with Andrew on Saturday'

Kevin Year 9

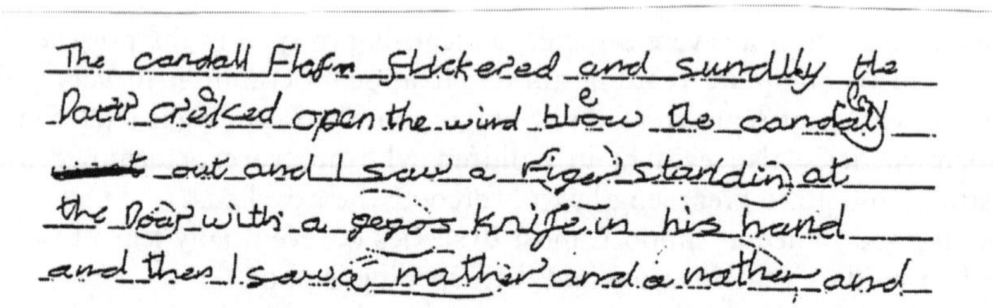

Figure 3.5b Some case examples of dyslexics' written work

DYSGRAPHIA (DCD – FINE)

With regard to dysgraphia, my studies indicate that the incidence is in the region of 30 per cent on a continuum from mild to severe (Montgomery, 2008) with boys 3 to 1 more prone to difficulties than girls. There was 1 per cent in the severest category.

Maria, Reception class, 5 years 10 months

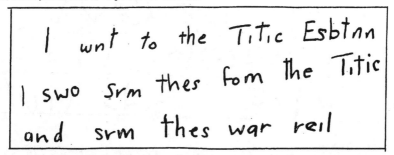

I wnt to the Titic Esbtnn
I swo srm thes fom the Titic
and srm thes war reil

'I went to the Titanic exhibition and saw some things from the Titanic and some of them were real'

Maria began reading self taught at 4 years. She is a fluent reader now, highly verbal with a wide vocabulary. She is bilingual in English and German.

Figure 3.6 Case example of a bright dysorthographic's writing

The ability to write neatly secures higher marks despite having poorer content, even though untidy writing from boys is more tolerated. Young very able children's thoughts may run much faster than their writing skills can cope with and so they will be criticised too, and again content can be ignored.

Writing at speed with reasonable legibility is a skill that is given too little attention, but lack of the skill can have a serious effect on school achievement. It results in lower SATs scores and degree classification. It is a hidden SEN and a hidden cause of UAch (Montgomery, 2000, 2009a).

In order to write well in examinations, a certain level of fluency and automaticity is needed in the basic skills of handwriting and spelling. In Year 7, the average writing speed in a 20-minute essay test is 13 words per minute (Montgomery, 2008). However, the speed required for learning success in the curriculum at that age is 17 to 20 words per minute, a speed that only a few per cent in the research achieved. In the most severe cases, pupils with DCD should not be required to learn to write in the Early Years but should be given a laptop to use and taught to touch-type.

D – RS + H research shows that 30 to 50 per cent of dyslexics also have handwriting difficulties. This makes their problems more intractable, so they easily get referred to specialist centres and the diagnosis is confused with dyslexia.

The writing speed of boys and girls was significantly different in my cohort analyses (ibid.). The group mean was 13.09 made up of boys 11.79 and girls 14.26. Could this account for the lower achievements of boys in school attainments? Does it account for their better achievements in subjects requiring less writing such as mathematics and science?

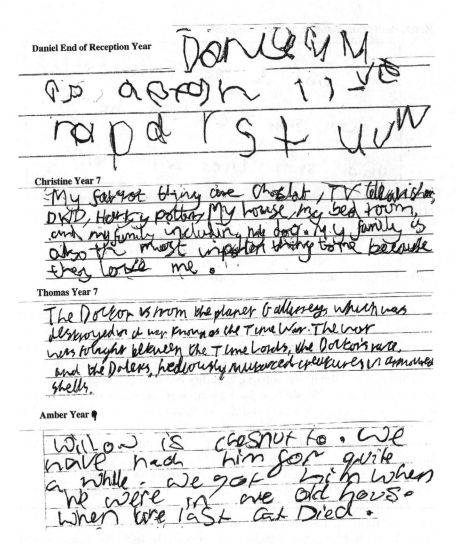

Figure 3.7 Case examples of handwriting coordination difficulties

PROVISION FOR DYSLEXIC DIFFICULTIES

Level one dyslexics need help in Reception to learn the alphabetic code. Evidence indicates that the 'deficit' lies in the left angular gyrus of the brain where sound-symbol and proprioceptive cues are linked.

The implications of this are that areas round the deficit problem need to be trained to take over the integrative function and this is harder work than if there was no deficit. It involves a process of overlearning for the first few symbols and sounds. This is a crucial period, for total confusion can set in if the pace is forced.

The essential route is to follow a multisensory, articulatory synthetic phonics process.

The best programmes with the right speed of introduction are:

1 Hickey's Language Training Programme (Augur and Brigg's 2nd edition, 1991, the version without the intrusion of the phoneme awareness training).

2 TRTS, 1994 (Teaching Reading Through Spelling Book 2 Foundations of the Programme, Cowdery *et al.*). This especially uses the articulatory awareness training and multisensory handwriting training essential to dyslexics.

In both programmes it is essential to follow the scheme very precisely. When the spelling pack work and dictations are omitted then the results are no better than other schemes.

When these programmes are used with First Level dyslexics after the age of six years the expected progress is: two years progress in each year with 2 × 50 minute sessions per week for matched pairs of pupils.

Level two dyslexics and dysorthographics – most bright dyslexics are discovered late and are able to read slowly but write and spell very poorly. They need second level intervention with a strategic approach to spelling that will also transfer to reading; I refer to this as Cognitive Process Strategies for Spelling (CPSS).

Twelve Cognitive Process Strategies for Spelling (CPSS) were implemented with second level dyslexics (Montgomery, 2007). Like the APSL programmes they were found to advance the spelling and reading skills by two years in each year with only a few minutes input each day. The essence is to use one of the twelve 'engage brain' strategies to correct the misspelling in the lexicon in the cerebrum and a linked cursive writing strategy to lay down a new memory in the motor memory store in the cerebellum. Look–cover–write–check on its own does not work because it does not correct the error in the lexicon.

The advantage of CPSS is that it can be used with all pupils in the form of mini-lessons in any subject involving writing.

Developmental coordination difficulties (DCD)

Dyspraxis is a difficulty with or an inability to motor plan, or put such a plan into fluent operation after a reasonable period of skill acquisition; for example, bead threading, shoelace tying and buttoning.

Between 5 to 10 per cent of the school population are estimated to have developmental coordination difficulties (DCD). The group includes those with gross motor difficulties and those who have fine coordination difficulties. The majority of pupils with gross motor difficulties will also have fine motor problems: a chronic symptom shows exercise books filled with scruffy, scrappy work loaded with crossings out and holes. Such pupils are not picked in team games and are frequently seriously bullied and can become the butt of jokes and blame.

Despite the ungainly behaviour, and perhaps a lack of control of emotional responses, the individual may be highly intelligent, trapped in a body that will not do as instructed unless specific training is given. If the writing is legible, the DCD is ignored but the pupil is condemned to UAch and is usually poor at spelling and maths.

DCD is easily identified when balance and coordination are required. DCD – Gross Motor affects the coordination of the general movements of the body including fine motor coordination. DCD – Fine Motor usually only affects the smaller more complex movements involving the hands. VMI – Visuo-motor integration affects coordination and spatial functions (see below).

The pupil with DCD – Gross Motor difficulties may:

- move too fast or too slow;
- show lack of control;
- be slow to react to signals;
- constantly fidget and fiddle with things;
- be easily distractible and inattentive;
- show organisational problems;
- have difficulties thinking through a plan of action and carrying it out;
- have difficulties in the recall of events and sequences as well as time;
- show inconsequential and impulsive behaviours;
- have difficulties with handwriting and copying from the board;
- slump and loll about in seat;
- walk down a corridor and veer to one wall;
- appear somewhat uncoordinated even when walking;
- show contra lateral body movements;
- constantly fall off apparatus and bump into things;
- lose books and other belongings;
- leave a trail of devastation;
- spill food and knock over tables and chairs;
- look as though 'has been pulled through a hedge backwards';
- have clothes and hair awry;
- in Early Years have problems with buttoning and tying shoelaces and changing for PE;
- find learning new skills challenging – for example, constantly falling off when learning to ride a bike or to skateboard.

VMI – VISUO-MOTOR INTEGRATION

Difficulties in this area may exist in the presence of adequate motor skills. The problem can be noticed when pupils follow a moving object with their eyes from right to left and their eyes jump as they attempt to cross the middle line. Pencils on the left will be picked up in the left hand and transferred to the right rather than using the right hand to cross the mid-line. Jigsaws and figure drawing may show difficulties as well as spatial location, far point copying and smooth text reading.

VERBAL OR ORAL DYSPRAXIA

This affects just the speech apparatus that is controlled by 100 different muscles. The child will need speech therapy to help the speech become intelligible and may need help in breathing, timing and sequencing with daily exercises. The following points need to be noted:

- Teachers need to ensure that others do not bully the child and no attempt should be made to correct the child's speech in front of others. Speech therapists advise that only the parents should correct it.
- Teachers are encouraged to help with particular sounds or remind the child of them.
- Reading is best taught to them using synthetic phonics methods.
- Cooperative learning methods are needed to promote social and communication skills.
- The talking curriculum is essential to promote talk and develop speech.
- Self-esteem needs support and praise.

PROVISION FOR PUPILS WITH DCD

The most important task is to consult the parents/carers and therapist involved in order to obtain advice for the particular needs. It may include programmes run by occupational therapists, remedial programmes implemented in PE and specialist training programmes. Swimming is often a recommended sport because it requires contra-lateral movements, balance and coordination.

Pupils with DCD will need some of the same provision as advised above for oral dyspraxia and, in addition, they need:

- work marked for content not neatness;
- less writing and more recording using other strategies;
- extra time for any copying, or access to photocopied notes;
- more time to learn new skills;
- gentle encouragement of better posture for longer periods;

- acceptance of writing style, with joining of letters taught from the outset so that the motor programme is established;
- consolidation of relevant sub-skills before the teaching of a new skill;
- to be seated close to the teacher or teaching assistant to ensure attention is properly focused;
- the school to be a 'DCD/Dyspraxia Friendly School'.

Attention deficit hyperactivity disorder (ADHD)

It is not uncommon for very bright children on entry to school to be absorbed by the newness of it all for a week or so and then to become bored by the routine, the sameness and slowness of everything. They begin to leak a nervous energy that has no intellectual outlet and teachers may try to over-correct this. The students are soon mislabelled 'hyperactive' and recommended for medication.

In ADHD, the disorder is manifested across all lessons and both at home and in school. It does not respond to the ordinary management behaviours such as reasoning, ignoring aversive behaviour and punishment. Even computer games may not keep the attention.

There are three main symptoms:

- *inattention* – in behavioural, ocular and postural set;
- *hyperactivity* – extreme and incessant mobility and restlessness;
- *impulsivity* – shouting and calling out, cannot take turns.

Overactivity does not always continue into adolescence and may be replaced by underactivity, inertia and lack of motivation. The pupil finds it difficult to undertake two tasks at the same time (multitasking).

ATTENTION DEFICIT DISORDER (ADD)

When the symptoms are present without the hyperactivity, the diagnosis is ADD. This condition is frequently overlooked as it can appear to be a case of dreaminess, disorganisation and quiet withdrawal: such a child may be easy to manage in a busy classroom, but little learning takes place. In pre-school, ADD is seen as a pattern of uninhibited curiosity and meddle-someness.

There tends to be continual trial and error learning, wandering away from the guarding adult, rash acceptance of strange adults and proneness to accidents. Studies show that those with hyperactivity are more likely to show aggressive behaviours whilst those without show a sluggish cognitive tempo.

ATTENTION DEFICIT IMPULSIVITY (ADI)

This aspect of the condition is given less attention because, like ADD, it is not so disruptive. It is often included as ADD. It shares the common features with ADD above: uninhibited activity and meddlesomeness, trial and error learning and inconsequential behaviour where the consequences of any action are not considered. Quiet withdrawal is not a feature.

Distinguishing between high energy levels of more able students and ADHD as a disorder is important. High energy level of more able learners is best seen in sudden and total concentration on a task of special interest or a computer game that a student with ADHD cannot maintain.

PROVISION IN ADHD

Medication such as Ritalin is often given for a temporary period whilst behaviour management programmes are implemented. It may not always calm down the behaviour but can improve concentration temporarily so that pupils can catch up with schoolwork. However, Ritalin can also depress the 'gifted' child's potential.

Another cause of ADHD may be an allergy to preservatives and additives in foods such as sausages, soft drinks and crisps – foods that most children enjoy. Yet others are allergic to chocolate, or cheese, or flour and milk protein, and a Feingold diet may be tried. Many schools have tuck-shops that now supply 'healthy eating snacks' and have found that learners are significantly calmer and more attentive in the afternoons.

Features of classrooms need to include:

- a calm environment low in distractions;
- low general work noise;
- sound-damping carpets;
- study carrels that help to focus attention;
- calming music in suitable lessons;
- periods of work interspersed with plenty of structured energy-consuming activity;
- 'Brain Gym' or physical activity exercises which can be helpful;
- calm and structured positive behaviour management programme (as in SEBD above);
- the pupil sitting close to the teacher so calming can take place quietly;
- cue signs to stop unwanted behaviours and impulsivity;
- a 'time-out' area so that the pupil can go there or be sent when s/he feels the need to avoid an outburst or avoid a confrontation.

We tend not to see the positive side of ADHD. For example, 'Bob' insisted that it made him a more exciting speaker, comedian and motivator; he claimed it was a gift. Perhaps it is the abnormal environment of classrooms full of confined children that prevents ADHD being used to advantage.

Learning disorders

AUTISTIC SPECTRUM DISORDERS (ASD)

These pupils have disorders, possibly carried on the genes, that cause them to have distinct patterns of difficulty in learning. In autism, Asperger's syndrome and pragmatic language disorders pupils may engage in behavioural rituals, lack social and communication skills, have severe difficulties in language and thinking and lack a theory of mind that prevents them from seeing things from another's point of view.

In autism isolated 'gifts' may be found in some 10 per cent of pupils, such as musical or artistic ability, or a facility with number calculations such as telling the day of the week in 1754 that was October 4th! They are called 'savants'. In most cases where IQ can be tested it does not rise much above 110.

Asperger's syndrome (AS) AS was originally thought to be high-functioning autism but now the characteristics are more clearly defined, the patterns may be different. In AS, there is serious impairment in social skills, there are repetitive behaviours and rituals, problems in fantasy and imaginative activities and play, concrete and literal comprehension of speech and a monotonous speech pattern. There is motor impairment in 50 to 90 per cent of cases. This latter is in contrast to autism in which there is usually good coordination even gracefulness, but severe impairment in other areas.

In AS, school achievement can be very good where the topics command a pupil's interest and require a large amount of factual or technical learning. Reading skills are generally good although 90 per cent with AS have writing difficulties.

Gifted adults with AS can be highly successful, holding important jobs especially if they have good self-care and a placid nature, but they often remain socially isolated and idiosyncratic. They appear to lack insight into their own thinking processes, understanding of the perspective of others and a theory of mind.

The child with AS can be differentiated from the 'ordinary gifted' by the following:

- pedantic seamless speech in which they run on mixing fact and personal detail;
- low tolerance to change, may ignore class and school routines completely;
- no understanding of humour, understanding is literal;

- clumsiness in 50–90 per cent;
- inappropriate affect and lack of insight – may laugh at a funeral;
- frequently have stereotypic behaviours and rituals (Niehart, 2000).

Early identification of the 'giftedness' may be vocabulary-based, for such learners are hyperlingual, but the comprehension shows deficits. In later school years, these pupils may be very successful in subjects requiring large amounts of factual material to be recalled. However, problems ensue if they are not interested in a subject, and they can make naive and overt insulting criticisms of a teacher's methods and personal attributes that are socially unacceptable.

Their behaviours can be rigid and resistant to change which brings them into conflict with other children and school staff, so that having been told to sit still and be quiet they continue questioning loudly or get up and walk around, oblivious to the instruction. Some engage in compulsive rituals such as shelf-tidying or hand-flapping, others are prone to sudden aggressive outbursts, temper tantrums, hyperactivity, anxiety or phobic attacks.

REFLECT

Case examples of AS

David is a bright 10-year-old who has just been diagnosed AS. He reads very well and has an excellent visual memory but his writing is very difficult to read. At the weekend he had been away camping with his parents and when asked 'What did you do when you were away?' He replied: 'I went to bed. I got dressed, ate breakfast' – AS literalism.

He does not understand jokes or sarcasm. He has difficulties in social situations with peers and his behaviour is immature for his age. He has many altercations in the playground and tends to play with younger children. He quickly becomes overexcited and then finds it difficult to calm down, engaging in much hand flapping and screaming. He does not like to join in class activities. For example, if the class is performing in assembly he refuses to take part and becomes very upset if someone tries to persuade him.

If his routine is interrupted, desks moved or a new teacher appears without notice, he gets very upset. When he enters the classroom, the first thing he does is check the date has been written on the top right-hand side of the board and becomes very frustrated if it is not. He insists the teacher writes it before they can begin lessons. Sometimes he completely refuses to listen or do any work at all.

When he tipped out the family's goldfish to clean the bowl and the fish died, he said his parents were very angry. He was unconcerned about it and had no idea at all why they should be so angry.

John attends mainstream secondary school. In lessons he makes frequent interruptions, asks inappropriate questions, does not accept that a conversation with a member of staff is finished when it is, has difficulties remaining in his seat and working in groups. When asked to do something he does not want to do he grumbles, looks angry and sometimes screams even at age 15. John is accelerated and given enrichment work in maths, physics, biology and modern foreign languages. In Year 8, he gains As in GCSE maths and physics. In Year 9 he gains A* in biology and A in French, yet his tutor has to develop a special learning programme for him to catch a bus to town, and another to manage his behaviour to prepare him for university.

Provision for pupils with Asperger's   Children with AS are very sensitive to teasing, but continually engage in precisely those asocial behaviours that provoke it. They all have different patterns of behaviour and no one teaching programme or intervention as yet has been defined.

However, a structured approach for AS students is needed:

- Teach the rules of interaction in conversation, such as, look at the person when they are speaking and only get ready to speak when they signal they are coming to a close by looking away and then looking back. How to 'chat up' a potential girlfriend was high on the 'wants lists' of youths with AS.
- Avoid bright lights, white walls, whiteboard and fluorescent lighting.
- Teach signal words such as 'No' and 'Finish' with a command sign.
- Avoid moving furniture once it has an established place.
- Ensure that there is careful warning of any change in the daily routine.
- Always speak directly to the pupil using his first name.
- Do not ask complex questions such as 'Why didn't you do this?'
- Avoid use of metaphors and fables, and reading for deeper meaning.
- Do not ask pupil to imagine something, or engage in fantasy and role play.
- Make good use of the strong visual memory that pupils with AS often have.
- Encourage staff to ignore what may seem rude comments and to explain the reason to other pupils so that they do not copy.
- Seek help for the handwriting difficulties, and if severe, give pupil a laptop.
- Teach the recognition of emotions and how other people may feel.

The more intelligent these pupils are the better they learn to manage their difficulties especially by adolescence, although they need specific and direct training in procedures, school rules and social protocols. They will have learned to cope with most regular and predictable demands of school, but they still need specific instructions for tasks that others learn naturally from experience. For example, specific teaching in how to go shopping, buy a ticket and take a bus and a train was necessary for a university applicant with AS to gain an Oxbridge place.

As well as Behaviour Management protocols, the Social Stories approach is widely recommended (Gray, 1990; Smith, 2002). A 'time out' area can also be helpful for times of stress and the Steer Report (DCFS, 2009a) recommends that all new schools should have such areas and rooms in the building plan.

SLI – SPECIFIC LANGUAGE IMPAIRMENT

Mild developmental dysphasia/specific language disorder   SLI is a set of language disorders originally termed developmental dysphasia. There are two major areas of deficit and a child may have either one or the other or both:

- *receptive* – in receptive difficulties the child has difficulty understanding spoken language.
- *expressive* – in expressive difficulties the child has problems in organising and executing speech to explain thought.

Receptive difficulties invariably lead to expressive problems as well but the reverse is not the case. As can be imagined SLI places a limitation on thinking and understanding that can be from mild to severe, and profound when no speech or understanding develops.

Children with SLI may only develop a vocabulary of about fifty words by the age of five years and there may be no grammatical use of speech such as, 'Want drink' the telegraphic speech typical of most two-year-olds.

Children with SLI need speech training support from the earliest age and the parents need to be trained in it as well. In addition, as with severe language deficits in autism, it may be necessary for them to be taught a sign language such as 'Makaton'.

The system of training needs to continue in the Early Years in school in a nurture group to focus on the language work in individual and a small group setting. If this systematic and strong support is given, it may be possible to mainstream some of these pupils.

Although pupils with SLI may find it very difficult to achieve well in schools because of the verbally based curriculum and pedagogy, they may, however, be exceptionally bright conceptually and perceptually in non-verbal areas. If they can draw, design, sing or perform well in an area such as sport, they can gain fulfilment, otherwise they can become despairing and depressed.

Their difficulties often attract bullying. Art, design and music can all be vehicles for expression of their high ability and they can engage in practical jobs that require minimal linguistic interaction.

SLCN – speech, language and communication needs   Significant numbers of children arrive at school with developmental language difficulties and delays: they have SLCN. These are usually milder conditions than SLI disorder. They may have learnt a number of useful but stereotyped verbal responses but they have difficulties in:

- ability to follow verbal instructions, usually missing first and last parts;
- completing work, are usually last;
- working individually or in groups.

They tend to:

- copy the behaviour of others;
- be easily led and follow inappropriate role models;
- withdraw from social situations;
- avoid eye contact.

In making provision for children with SCLN, three important principles are to:

- engage in inclusive teaching;
- ensure that the talking curriculum is fully exploited to develop their speech and language skills;
- promote collaborative learning to develop social and communication skills.

Nurture groups of about eight to ten pupils can be very beneficial to such children and the aim is to enable them to join their mainstream class as soon as possible. Only when they communicate well can they begin to realise their potential. In addition, the co-occurrence of SLCN and SEBD has been found to be 55–100 per cent and nurture groups can be designed to address both needs.

If all Reception class sizes were cut down to a maximum of fifteen pupils, this would have a significant impact on the nature and quality of the speech and language work that can be developed. It would give disadvantaged pupils an early opportunity to achieve their potential and compete on equal terms with peers.

The new review of the primary curriculum by Sir Jim Rose (Rose, 2009) suggesting there should be six broad areas of learning could also contribute to lifting achievement since its first area is 'understanding English, communication and language'.

Conclusion

The successful schools in the case-study research project have provided the context for this chapter. They are inclusive schools with an extensive and an enriching curriculum and varied teaching provision. They contain highly skilled teachers who are concerned to address the needs of all their children. All the schools engaged in systematic and thorough continuing professional development and had as good provision for the pupils with special needs as for those with giftedness and talents.

Their identification procedures were thorough, using sensitive teacher assessment alongside appropriate quantitative tests that were carefully analysed. In the Early Years classrooms there were systematic but flexible literacy teaching schemes that used guidelines such as Ruth Miskin's programme and Jolly Phonics. Language and thinking were priorities and the cognitive and talking curricula were well in evidence.

Positive behaviour management policies were implemented and all levels of relevant provision were noted from mentoring projects to many very active clubs and societies, whole-school outings, master classes and extensive parental and community involvement. The schools were hives of energy and purposeful activity.

The individual case studies and the more detailed advice regarding double exceptionality, however, come from my research and teaching for the Learning Difficulties Research Project (LDRP) and from teachers studying on my masters' programmes. This is because such evidence takes years rather than days to collect.

Two themes dominate this chapter: first, teachers need to fully understand the complexities of double exceptionality; and, second, they need to understand the values of teaching and learning that develop cognitive challenge and stretch and communication skills.

The complex links of Double Exceptionality

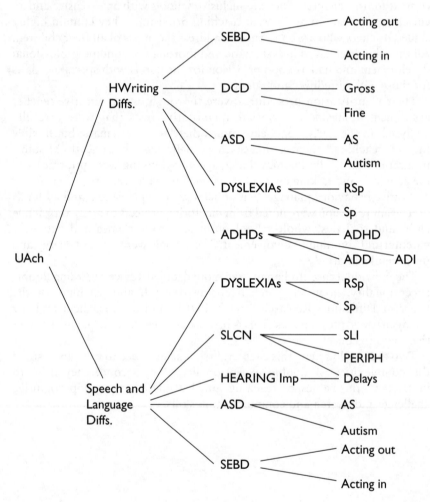

Figure 3.8 Summary concept map 3

References and further reading

Butterworth, B. (2006) BBC Radio Four interview: *The Today Programme*, 2 April. Also: *Dyscalculia Screener*. Online: www.dyslexiaaction.org.

DCFS (2009a) *Learning Behaviour: The Report of the Practitioner Group on School Behaviour and Discipline: The Steer Report.* London: DfES.

DCFS (2009b) *Statistics in Education 2007–2008.* London: DfES.

DfEE (1999) *Excellence in Cities.* London: DfEE.

DfES (2004–09) *Personalising Learning: A Practical Guide.* Online: www.teacher net.gov.uk.publications.

Freeman, J. (1991) *Gifted Children Growing Up.* London: Cassell.

Gray, L. (1990) *Original Social Story Book.* New York: Future Horizons.

Hallam, S. (2002) *Ability Grouping in Schools.* London: Institute of Education Publications.

Hayden, S. and Jordan, E. (2004) *Language for Learning.* London: David Fulton.

Higgins, P. (2002) 'Teaching and learning in the foundation subjects: An overview of the Key Stage 3 strand', *Curriculum Briefing*, 1 (1): 3–6.

Montgomery, D. (ed.) (2009a) *Able, Gifted and Talented Underachievers.* Oxford: Wiley/Blackwell.

Montgomery, D. (2009b) *Mathematical Difficulties and Dyscalculia.* Maldon: Learning Difficulties Research Project.

Montgomery, D. (2008) 'Cohort analysis of writing in Year 7 after 2, 4, and 7 years of the National Literacy Strategy', *Support for Learning,* 23 (1): 3–11.

Montgomery, D. (2007) *Spelling, Handwriting and Dyslexia.* London: Routledge.

Montgomery, D. (ed.) (2003) *Gifted and Talented with Special Educational Needs: Double Exceptionality.* London: David Fulton.

Montgomery, D. (2002) *Helping Teachers Improve through Classroom Observation.* 2nd edition. London: David Fulton.

Montgomery, D. (ed.) (2000) *Able Underachievers.* London: Whurr.

Montgomery, D. (1999) 'Supporting "able misfits" in the primary classroom', in P. Cooper (ed.) *Understanding and Supporting Children with Emotional and Behavioural Difficulties.* London: Jessica Kingsley, pp. 183–200.

Montgomery, D. (1997) *Spelling: Remedial Strategies.* London: Cassell.

Niehart, M. (2000) 'Gifted children with Asperger Syndrome', *Gifted Child Quarterly,* 44 (4): 222–230.

Raven, J. C. (2008) *Raven's Progressive Matrices.* London: Pearson Assessment.

Rayner, S. (1998) 'Educating pupils with emotional and behaviour difficulties "Pedagogy is the key"', *Emotional and Behavioural Difficulties,* 4 (3): 44–51.

Rose, J., Sir (2009) *Independent Review of the Primary Curriculum: Final Report.* Nottingham: DCFS.

Shayer, M. and Adey, P. (eds) (2002) *Learning Intelligence: Cognitive Acceleration across the Curriculum from 3 to 25 years.* Milton Keynes: OU Press.

Silverman L. K. (2004) 'Poor handwriting: a major cause of underachievement'. Online: www.gifteddevelopment.com/Articles/vsl/v37.pdf (accessed April 2007).

Sisk, D. (2003) 'Gifted with behaviour disorders: marching to a different drummer', in D. Montgomery (ed.) *Gifted and Talented Children with SEN.* London: David Fulton, pp. 131–54.

Smith, L. (2002) 'An investigation of children having EBD with dyslexic type difficulties in 2 Special Schools and a Pupil Referral list'. Unpublished dissertation, London Middlesex University.

Wallace, B., Fitton, S. Leyden, S., Montgomery, D, Pomerantz, M. and Winstanley, C. (2007) *Raising the Achievement of Able, Gifted and Talented Pupils within an Inclusive School Framework: Guidelines for Schools to Audit and Extend Existing Best Practice.* Oxford: National Association for Able Children in Education. Obtainable from: publications@nace.co.uk.

Wallace, B. (2000) *Teaching the Very Able Child.* London: David Fulton.

Useful websites

www.addiss.org.uk	ADDISS, ADHD information services
www.afasic.org.uk	AFASIC, Association for all Speech Impaired Children
www.bdadyslexia.org.uk	The British Dyslexia Association
www.dyslexia-action.org.uk	Dyslexia Action, includes the Dyslexia institute
www.dyspraxiafoundation.org.uk	The Dyspraxia Foundation
www.ican.org.uk	Supporting the development of speech, language and communication skills in all children
www.nace.co.uk	The National Association for Able Children in Education
www.nas.org.uk	The National Autistic Society
www.nha-handwriting.org.uk	The National Handwriting Association
www.sapere.org.uk	Society for Advancing Philosophical Enquiry and Reflection in Education
www.sebda.org	An association for promoting services for children and young people with SEBD
www.speechmark.net	Resources and publications
www.tascwheel.com	Thinking Actively in a Social Society

Chapter 4

Providing challenging opportunities in the classroom

Carrie Winstanley

Introduction

The concept of challenge is clearly vital in supporting able children and keeping them motivated in school. This chapter starts by considering answers to the following questions:

- What is challenge?
- How can teachers ensure equality of challenge?
- How is challenge essential?
- What are the barriers to challenge?

The second half of the chapter looks at practical responses to providing challenge, focusing on some key aspects of good practice:

- cognitive challenge through appropriate questioning;
- thinking skills and philosophy;
- independent project work.

Part 1: all about challenge

Challenge is currently a buzz-word in education. It is often used, but rarely defined. It might seem reasonable to assume that we share an understanding of such a common word, but since the term is so widely used, it is worth checking that it is being used coherently in the range of different contexts in which it is found. What is challenging to one person is not necessarily difficult for someone else and so some aspects of challenge must be personal.

Most would agree that challenge is synonymous with some of the following terms: 'demanding', 'arduous', 'strenuous', 'testing' and 'complicated'. The nuances of each word are relevant; however, something that is 'arduous' is not particularly appealing. Some might argue that challenge can come from the simplest of tasks, rendering 'complicated' erroneous. People who like learning would use positive words such as 'stimulating' whilst those who have had more negative experiences may prefer to describe academic challenge as 'intractable' or 'gruelling'.

Perhaps it is not possible to make any clear statements about the nature of challenge that can be broadly applicable. However, most people would agree that some tasks are inherently more complex than others. It is generally going to be more difficult to build a house than to put up a shelf and easier to cook for two than to cater for 300.

Pupils who report satisfaction with their schooling experience often cite 'appropriate challenge' as a reason for their fulfilment. Their teachers have been successful in understanding and providing challenge and so there must be some principles of challenge that can be extrapolated and applied to different contexts (see Wallace *et al.*, 2007; Winstanley, forthcoming).

A useful task is to consider ideas to do with challenge and to review colleagues' understandings of the concept. See Box 4.1 for suggested points for reflection and discussion.

Box 4.1 Thinking about you as an individual and a teacher

- What has been your most significant personal life challenge?
- What subject did you find most challenging at school? Why?
- Do you still seek challenge? If so, how do you go about this search?
- How do you feel when you have overcome challenge?
- How can you tell when you have hit the right note in challenging your pupils? How can you tell when they are not challenged?
- (This can be a bit controversial!) Are some curriculum subjects inherently more challenging than others?
- What's the difference between a challenging task and simply being unprepared or inexperienced?

How can teachers ensure equality of challenge?

Many different aspects of equality are important in schooling – equality of opportunity, equality of resources and sometimes even equality of outcomes. For more able children, even where they may be treated equally and fairly in many ways, they can often lack the one aspect of equality they most crave: equality of challenge from a personal perspective (Winstanley, 2004). What is striking about the case-study schools that have inspired this text is that they all value challenge very highly and make special efforts to ensure equality of personal challenge. As well as teachers monitoring levels of challenge, pupils are often invited to discuss their own thoughts and feelings about their levels of challenge.

To a certain extent, challenge is about 'nudging' pupils out of their comfort zone. Able pupils come in many varieties, and some of those who tend to conform and coast are particularly in need of being encouraged beyond where they are comfortable. One way to do this is to persuade such pupils to try out activities in areas that might not be their clear first choice.

Thinking about your pupils, consider who tends to play it safe by sticking to what they know they can already do. Think about the questions in Box 4.2 as honestly as you can!

REFLECT

Box 4.2 Persuading pupils to take risks in learning

- How do non-risk-takers compare with the risk-takers who have a go at anything presented to them, even if they are likely to fail?
- Could you do more to encourage the 'comfortably' able to explore uncharted territory?
- Are you comfortable with pupils failing to complete set tasks or producing disappointing results from time to time?
- How can you ensure that you are not sending mixed messages about trying things out no matter the outcome, whilst maintaining high standards?

Children are entitled to an education based on their needs. Just as they have an entitlement to be helped to achieve reasonable standards of numeracy and literacy, they should also receive a fair chance of being treated with respect and securing satisfying employment. Pupils should have support for their problems, freedom to develop socially, personally and intellectually but also the opportunities to be challenged, stimulated and engaged. This last aspect is less obvious than the preceding requirements and is viewed as a luxury by some practitioners who are happy to let the able cater for themselves, declaring specific support to be some kind of pandering to elitist principles.

Underachievers and children with multiple exceptionalities

All children in schools should be provided with an enabling education that allows the development of their talents. This is particularly significant with underachieving able pupils who tend to exhibit a large gap between their actual and potential achievements.

At first sight, able pupils seem unlikely candidates for additional provision as their needs are not often obvious *deficit* needs. However, within the population of highly able children, there are many with additional special needs, such as support for coping with a sensory impairment, disability or learning difficulty. These pupils are variously described as having multiple exceptionalities or dyssynchronous development. Often, their difficulties are catered for, to a greater or lesser extent, by schools' legal obligations to provide support. However, high ability is rarely considered as a special educational need, falling outside of government regulations. We are left with able children with learning problems who have their difficulties addressed, but their high abilities ignored. (See Chapter 3 on dual and multiple exceptionalities.)

REFLECT

• Have you included children with difficulties such as dyslexia, dyspraxia and attention deficit disorder on your register of able children?
• How effective is your school in providing support for their difficulties whilst also stretching their areas of strength?

What about highly able pupils without particular problems? Depending on their type of abilities and their school, it is necessary to provide opportunities beyond the usual offer of the school. No matter the nature of the able child (with or without additional problems; all-round able or specialist; extremely capable or more modestly able, etc.), tasks have to help pupils sustain interest and maintain motivation. Wherever possible, tasks should be intrinsically challenging. This is especially the case if pupils cannot see obvious extrinsic rewards or clear purpose for the activities in question.

Why is challenge essential?

The notion of challenge emerges from all the case studies of the twelve successful schools, and, consequently, best practice can be distilled from these findings. Schools report a general ethos that encourages challenge, and this is fully and openly supported by school management. In all cases this policy is made explicit in the school prospectus and is presented as part of the core school values.

Discuss the following quotations from pupils and teachers in the case-study schools, and compare them with similar quotations that might possibly come from your school.

REFLECT

> The ethos has changed towards gifted and talented youngsters; there has been a move away from playing safe to creating a culture of exciting and innovative challenge for all pupils.

It's better to be challenged and fail rather than not being challenged at all.

Teachers challenge pupils to take risks and support them when things go wrong; this has helped the pupils build self-confidence and self-belief, challenging their thinking and at the same time motivating and engaging them.

Class teachers are very aware of the different abilities of the children they teach and plan work accordingly. They work very hard to provide the appropriate level of work for children, ensuring that all are challenged.

What issues arise with regard to inclusion and identification?

Providing challenge helps to identify high ability. Through a range of complex tasks and activities, children can demonstrate their strengths and propensities. In the case-study schools, rising to a particular challenge is one key identifying factor in picking up on unusual abilities within both gifted and general populations. A common feature of less successful schools is that they have a fixed approach as to who constitutes the highly able cohort and then they restrict challenging activities to that group, failing to allow some pupils to shine.

If children are restricted in their capacity to partake in an activity through a minority language for example, or a physical disability, adjustments must be made to the tasks allowing children to express their skills and talents. Fair challenge for all is essential to allow children to show what they can do.

What issues arise with regard to provision?

Any phase of education in which transition occurs can potentially be a time when continuity of challenge is broken, but it can also be an opportunity. Where schools have succeeded in developing smooth transition practices, this has been the consequence of involving the community and other networks to support children and to offer them the chance to reach beyond what their current context offers. So, for both secondary and primary pupils, this can mean links with an expert or a university, or a special mentor, either actual or virtual.

Out-of-hours learning is also highlighted in all the case studies and the range of opportunities is rich and diverse. These opportunities contribute to a positive ethos and help minimise underachievement through encouraging everyone to find a way to express their interests and abilities and to have these valued by the school and wider community.

Assessment for Learning (AfL) is also cited as an opening for increased challenge. Through discussing targets, monitoring progress and in-depth feedback, teachers and pupils are able to match challenge more closely to learning needs.

How can we classify different types of underachievement?

When considering how challenge is essential, it is important to consider the typologies of underachieving able pupils usually found among the hetero-geneous population of highly able children and young people in schools. (For more detail of the typologies, refer back to Chapter 1.)

In discussion with colleagues and with reference to pupils in your care, consider how challenge is vital to enhance the learning experience. You can fill in the empty column in Table 4.1 which raises questions about the consequences of failing to challenge these pupils:

Table 4.1 Possible consequence of lack of challenge

Pupil typology	Description	Specific type of challenge required	Dangers of failing to challenge
Conforming coasters	Teacher pleasers; can rest on laurels	Anything to move them out of their comfort zone	
Impatient inattentives	Butterfly learners, often fail to complete tasks	Setting their own challenge keeps motivation. Learning how to stay on course is important	
Apathetic non-engagers	Do not contribute or engage effectively	Real-life problems sustain interest	
Risk avoiders	Stick to what they have proven they can manage	Learning responsibility and resilience	
Disaffected disengaged	Complain and disrupt	Tasks should require group work for integration, but must be relevant, with a sense of ownership	
Multiply exceptional	Highly able, with learning problems, disability or sensory impairments	Learning support where required, but sufficient challenge as well	

What are the barriers to challenge?

In Chapter 1, one of the *barriers* to learning is identified as lack of challenge. Box 1.4 on page 16 lists various aspects. This chapter uses the list to structure a discussion of challenge for highly able children, offering some practical ideas. The practice is based on the case studies from the original case-study project and picks out some of the more successful and popular strategies designed to ensure challenge is embedded in schools through building on existing positive practice.

As you review the sections below, keep in mind your own school situation and note where you recognise the successes and barriers pertinent to your own situation.

REFLECT

Barriers to challenge: perceived lack of relevance in the curriculum

Any national curriculum can present learners with opportunities, but can also have limits with regards to its scope. The National Curriculum in the UK has evolved through various stages, and over its two decades it has slowly loosened its grip on some areas of study, whilst tightening up on others.

To see where the challenge (or lack of challenge) originates, the basis of the curriculum needs scrutiny. The underlying assumptions of the English curriculum are broadly based on the sequential nature of Piagetian understandings of how children learn and develop cognitively; this can deny younger pupils the opportunities for exploring more abstract ideas. Able children can easily accelerate beyond concrete experiential learning and can cope with abstract ideas.

If teachers can free themselves from the habit of assuming that young children's understanding must move sequentially from the concrete to the abstract, they are more likely to provide appropriate challenge for the more able. The development of tasks in the curriculum generally adheres (more or less rigidly, depending on the subject) to the move from local to global, personal to generalised, practical to conceptual, active to theoretical. More able pupils may not always work in that linear direction. When useful extension and enrichment tasks are planned, they need to be used as the *starting point*, rather than the *follow-up*, if challenge is to be assured.

For older pupils, the lack of relevance usually revolves around the sense of the pointlessness of many tasks. By discussing the relevance and purpose of learning objectives, this problem can be reduced. Involving pupils in planning their own work has a two-fold benefit: a) to avoid irrelevance through the pupils choosing what they feel is relevant to their lives; and b) providing a sense of ownership that provides overwhelming motivation which in turn renders perceived irrelevance less of a factor.

Barriers to challenge: focus on facts rather than problem-solving

Where pupils are required to memorise facts and regurgitate ideas, they often remain unchallenged. Thinking that reaches higher levels of complexity is clearly central to finding a suitable offer for able learners, but this should not be an optional add-on.

Sometimes confusion arises when people suggest that there should not be a focus on facts and knowledge: it is not that there should be no subjects or information taught, and it is not that facts and concepts should be eradicated. The development of skills is an empty affair if it is content-free, since the result is a series of exercises lacking substance. When pupils complain of a focus on facts, they are bemoaning the thin regurgitation of knowledge often required by simplistic tasks, not rejecting the importance of facts and information. Problem-solving scenarios provide interesting contexts for learning whilst still requiring the use and understanding of knowledge.

A NOTE ON PROBLEM-BASED LEARNING (PBL)

Formal problem-based learning exists as a teaching style or perhaps even a movement in education, and teachers can be put off by the level of theory and discussion about the objectives that can accompany its description and associated tips. PBL consists of students collaboratively solving problems and then reflecting on the experience. In this method, pupils are facilitating their own learning and working together. Ultimately, it can be more appropriate for some teachers to adopt aspects of this method (such as the open-ended setting of tasks) without undertaking major collaborative projects.

Barriers to challenge: lack of learning through real-life experience

In school, it helps to sustain motivation if tasks have currency and impact. Where something turns on the learning, or where the exercise has a valued outcome, children need to *see* its value (whether it is intrinsic or extrinsic). A real-life task encourages active participation and this generates excitement and satisfaction through outcomes that are demonstrable and tangible.

Various models for experiential learning exist, mostly presented in a circular form with interconnecting arrows. The main components tend to incorporate:

- experience/activity/experimentation (always concrete);
- processing the experience/reflection and discussion – initially individually or in small groups/pairs;
- conceptualising the activity/abstracting key aspects;
- generalisation and application – explicit links to different contexts;
- sometimes an optional additional layer of reflection or recording of the overall cycle is included.

Another dimension of real-life learning is the focus on other aspects of development beyond the cognitive. Affective aspects are important, incorporating self-esteem, self-confidence, attitudes, values and even ethical issues. (See Chapter 2 with regard to the importance of the affective aspects of development and motivation.)

Some interesting work is emerging (usually internet-based) about the technology of 'Second Life' (SL) for educational purposes (for people over age 13 years only) and SL is a free-to-access virtual world in which people can participate in a range of virtual activities, individually and in groups (www.secondlife.com). It allows for complex social interaction and simulations with apparently impactful consequences. At the time of writing, educational possibilities are relatively embryonic, but already medical students have access to simulated doctor–patient scenarios and trainee teachers can work in simulated schools. For teenagers, possibilities are being developed for simulations such as field trips to ancient Rome and national museums and galleries have virtual alternatives, such as San Francisco's renowned science 'Exploratorium' (www.exploratorium.edu/worlds/secondlife/).

In terms of more commonplace responses to involving children in their own work planning, ideas such as the Total Curriculum (KS3) can incorporate increased pupil investment in their own tasks and end projects. This revamping of the curriculum has an emphasis on visits and trips, links with universities and business and also encourages pupils to feel more keenly part of their learning. (See Chapter 5 on students as researchers.)

Barriers to challenge: endless repetition of skills and content

The most soul-destroying phrase for an able child to hear is 'Well done. Now, carry on with more of the examples/questions'. Having to do 'more of the same' is so much of an anti-reward or punishment that able learners pick up a message that there is little point in expressing their ability.

Solving this problem is about having interesting tasks prepared, letting pupils decide for themselves what they might do and making it clear what is essential so that starting and end points are logical and matched to abilities and experience.

Use Box 4.3 to think about how you plan the tasks pupils need to accomplish in order to meet required objectives. To ensure challenge, pupils only need to demonstrate that they have met the requisite levels rather than completing all the set tasks. In this example, 'must' and 'should' are implied and an able writer can be directed to the 'could' section as their starting point.

To avoid repetition, the most useful action a teacher can take is to help pupils learn how best to find their own starting level for an activity and trust them to be accurate. This needs monitoring, but able pupils tend to crave challenge and if the ethos encourages the expression of abilities, this technique can be very helpful.

REFLECT

Box 4.3 Must/Should/Could – example from storywriting

Objectives

1   To capture the reader's attention.
2   To structure the story logically.
3   To hone use of adjectives.

Task

Using one of the story starters (provide opening paragraphs), write the next three paragraphs, taking up the story, but not finishing it completely.

When you are writing, you must:

• Write in full, correctly punctuated sentences.
• Move the story on by introducing a new character or event.
• Use adjectives to describe the new event or character.

When you are writing, you should:

• Have something intriguing about your new character or event that you will hold back for later in the story.
• Use alliteration to spice up your writing.
• Use the thesaurus to help you find some new words.

When you are writing, you could:

• Redraft your work to make it succinct.
• Vary your length of sentences.
• Include similes and metaphor.

Barriers to challenge: lack of ownership and control

It can be threatening to teachers to surrender to pupils some of their control over setting tasks and activities. But this shift of power can be very helpful as it increases engagement, provides a sense of ownership and allows pupils to learn how to negotiate and make decisions. Various factors help to make children more engaged, including choice, control and collaboration with peers.

Consider the list in Box 4.4 (adapted from the findings of Powell *et al.*, 2006). The list summarises teachers' strategies for effectively engaging pupils through allowing them control over their learning. How do these apply to your own context?

Box 4.4 Some strategies for effectively engaging pupils

- Allowing pupils choice to select tasks and texts so they choose what they find interesting and personally relevant.
- Appropriately tailored tasks are provided, with gradually withdrawn support and structure for learning.
- Pupils share in the decision-making process, set their own goals and take responsibility for their own development.
- Social interaction is encouraged, enabling mutual learning support.
- Discussing learning objectives so that pupils make sense of what they are learning.
- Providing a positive, encouraging ethos.

Minimising repetition of skills and increasing student sense of ownership are both tackled effectively through the Assessment for Learning (AfL) strategies. Where these are correctly and thoughtfully applied, children should be taking on tasks at the right level; they have ownership and can see the value of participating and completing.

Barriers to challenge: lack of recognition of personal strengths

In order to challenge pupils through appropriate task-setting, teachers need to understand their pupils. One way to do this is to reduce the range of abilities in any one class through setting. This need not be a permanent arrangement: setting can be used in some subjects only and it needs to be applied flexibly with as much opportunity for movement in and out of sets as is practically possible.

Really getting to know pupils' strengths and areas for support comes from working with them over time in different circumstances and in different atmospheres. Checklists and inventories of personal characteristics can also be used. These abound in the field of gifted education and are of variable value. One that stands out, however, is the Nebraska Starry Night protocol. It has a wider range of behavioural elements than most checklists and extends to affective and personality areas, rather than being restricted to cognitive abilities and approaches to tasks.

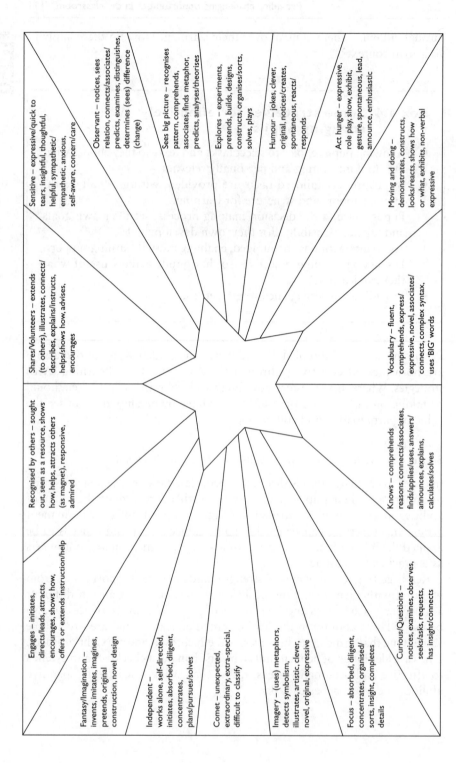

Sensitive – expressive/quick to tears, insightful, thoughtful, helpful, sympathetic/empathetic, anxious, self-aware, concern/care

Observant – notices, sees relation, connects/associates/predicts, examines, distinguishes, determines (sees) difference (change)

Sees big picture – recognises pattern, comprehends, associates, finds metaphor, predicts, analyses/theorises

Explores – experiments, pretends, builds, designs, constructs, organises/sorts, solves, plays

Humour – jokes, clever, original, notices/creates, spontaneous, reacts/responds

Act hunger – expressive, role play, show, exhibit, gesture, spontaneous, lead, announce, enthusiastic

Moving and doing – demonstrates, constructs, looks/reacts, shows how or what, exhibits, non-verbal expressive

Engages – initiates, directs/leads, attracts, encourages, shows how, offers or extends instruction/help

Shares/Volunteers – extends (to others), illustrates, connects/describes, explains/instructs, helps/shows how, advises, encourages

Recognised by others – sought out, seen as a resource, shows how, helps, attracts others (as magnet), responsive, admired

Vocabulary – fluent, comprehends, express/expressive, novel, associates/connects, complex syntax, uses 'BIG' words

Knows – comprehends reasons, connects/associates, finds/applies/uses, answers/announces, explains, calculates/solves

Fantasy/Imagination – invents, imitates, imagines, pretends, original construction, novel design

Independent – works alone, self-directed, initiates, absorbed, diligent, concentrates, plans/pursues/solves

Comet – unexpected, extraordinary, extra-special, difficult to classify

Imagery – (uses) metaphors, detects symbolism, illustrates, artistic, clever, novel, original, expressive

Focus – absorbed, diligent, concentrates, organised/sorts, insight, completes details

Curious/Questions – notices, examines, observes, seeks/asks, requests, has insight/connects

Figure 4.1 Behavioural elements from 'Nebraska Starry Night' (adapted from Griffin and McKenzie, 1992)

Barriers to challenge: curriculum subjects

Within the case studies of schools, no one curriculum area has emerged as vital for more able children since challenge is a personal matter; what is easy for some is difficult for others. Some writers in the field of gifted and talented education have argued that some subjects have components that make them more inherently challenging (see, for example, Van Tassel-Baska (2004) on classics). However, teachers and pupils we met in the case-study schools did not agree with this notion, since challenge was described not in terms of content, but in terms of how the content is presented.

However, for reasons of resources, geography and economics, some curriculum subjects are unavailable to pupils. Where this offends against equality of opportunity and challenge, school managers and local authorities need to be aware of all pupils' needs and it is usually teachers and parents who are best placed to raise these concerns.

Conclusion to Part I

It is vital to lift the barriers to challenge in schools. Consider the following two comments about the consequences of lack of challenge. Do you agree?

> Boredom and lack of cognitive challenge in the daily curriculum is playing a more significant role in causing pupils across the ability range to become disaffected than was originally suspected . . . more pupils, including the highly able and the more creative, are rejecting such 'schooling' and are switching off.
>
> (Montgomery, 2000:130–1)

> [W]hen lessons are too easy they [children] lose the satisfaction of tackling and resolving problems. To compensate, they may deliberately provoke disturbance, either in their own minds or among others in the classroom, just to taste the spice of stimulation.
>
> (Freeman, 1997: 488)

To complete this section, think for a moment about the role of management in helping teachers maintain their high standards of providing challenge. In most of the schools we visited, discussion and support documents about planning for challenge are regularly provided. One case-study school reports:

> Over 190 lesson observations were carried out during the past year, all of which include a report on the level of challenge and opportunities for extension. Performance Management interviews include a focus on G + T as well as other learning needs.

Part 2: key aspects of challenge

All of the points raised so far are important and contribute to making the school experience relevant for children. Three key ideas emerge, however, that merit a sharper focus and further detail:

- cognitive challenge through appropriate questioning;
- thinking skills and philosophy with children;
- independent project work.

The rest of the chapter will devote further attention to these areas, with a practical slant.

How important are cognitive challenge and questioning?

Accomplished teachers adapt their task-setting to reflect the different levels of ability among learners, providing appropriate cognitive challenge that really engages pupils. This notion of differentiation is not new in teaching, but in the case studies it is cited by pupils and teachers alike as a vital response to catering for highly able pupils. What stands out in the most successful schools is how personalised differentiated provision is:

> perceived as integral to whole-school planning . . . as such, differentiation is not a series of bolt-on exercises without coherence and sound educational rationale.
>
> (Wallace *et al.*, 2007: 13)

Schools use a range of varied methods, embedded in classroom practice:

> Through the differentiation, extension and enrichment strategies in lessons, teachers are able to use curriculum-based assessment to extend the pupils' range of skills and to further develop the cognitive stretch in targeting thinking and questioning skills.
>
> (ibid.: 18)

How useful is Bloom's Taxonomy?

Most teachers who have attended any kind of in-service training about helping highly able children will have come across Bloom's Taxonomy. It is a really useful way to think about the level of challenge for pupils, but it can be a rather tired response to the needs of pupils, depending on how it is used.

Most often in books and seminars, the cognitive domain of Bloom's work is presented as a stand-alone taxonomy, with little or no regard paid to the affective (or psychomotor/skills) aspects that Bloom also presented. The derivative understanding from the taxonomy is that you can plan questions from the most basic up to the highest level, thereby challenging the most able at the 'higher' levels. In some cases this can be a useful tactic, but it is a rather simplified and corrupted interpretation of the value of the taxonomy. Bloom was distinguishing between different types of questions to which *all* children can respond at differing levels. He was not creating a sequential hierarchy of questions in which only the more able could respond at the 'higher' levels.

The key point is that a teacher can use the taxonomies to improve the quality and variety of questioning in the classroom; the other domains have an impact on this as well. Tables 4.2 and 4.3 summarise the two main aspects of Bloom's work to show the depth and breadth that can be achieved. I then present a slightly different approach to questioning that owes much to Bloom, but presents a more nuanced understanding of how children benefit from teachers' different questions.

Table 4.2 The cognitive domain (most advanced at top of table)

Six categories	Questions	Verbs
Evaluation: making judgements	Which is the best for the purpose? What should the criteria be . . .?	Evaluating critiquing justifying judging proving valuing monitoring
Synthesis: creating meaningful structures from diverse elements	How can you better the design of . . .? What other ways are there to . . .?	Imagining creating generating hypothesising inventing constructing adapting improving
Analysis: discriminating between facts and inferences to present meaningful understandings	Which are the key factors in . . .? How does x match up to y?	Attributing contrasting comparing deconstructing investigating
Application: using concepts in different contexts	How can you use this information to help solve x?	Creating models ordering linking to new situations implementing
Comprehension: restating ideas to show understanding	Illustrate how x? In your own words, what is meant by x? Why?	Interpreting exemplifying illustrating inferring reorganising classifying generalising summarising
Knowledge: recalling information or ideas	List all the factors for x. Who? Where? What? Which? When?	Collecting information recording observing identifying recalling defining

Note: adapted from a range of sources, including teacher workshops and INSET days.

Table 4.3 The affective domain (most advanced at top of table)

Five categories	Examples of behaviours	Key verbs
Characterisation: internalising values and embracing a value system that affects behaviour	Self-reliance within independent working; effective cooperative group activities and teamwork; objective approaches taken to problem solving; relies on evidence to make judgements. (All demonstrated consistently.)	Discriminates, influences, listens, modifies, proposes, qualifies, questions, revises, serves, solves, verifies
Organisation: developing a revised value system based on consideration of multiple views	Recognises the balance between freedom and responsibility; accepts responsibility for own behaviour and actions; prioritises effectively.	Alters, arranges, combines, compares, completes, defends, explains, modifies, prepares, relates, theorises, examines, balances
Valuing: committing to a position and presenting an attitude and viewpoint	Sensitive towards individual differences; ability to solve problems; follows through plans with commitment.	Completes, demonstrates, differentiates, explains, follows, forms, initiates, invites, joins, justifies, proposes, reads, reports, selects, shares, studies, works, supports, debates
Responding: active interest and participation by the learner	Participates in class discussions; questions ideas and information appropriately to increase understanding.	Answers, assists, conforms, discusses, helps, labels, performs, practises, presents, reads, recites, reports, selects, tells, writes, follows, commends
Receiving: developing awareness and paying attention	Listen to others with respect; takes note of new ideas and people.	Asks, chooses, describes, follows, gives, holds, identifies, locates, names, points to, selects, sits, erects, replies, uses, differentiates, accept, listens for, responds to

Note: adapted from a range of sources, including teacher workshops, INSET days and Bloom's *Affective Taxonomy* (Anderson and Krathwohl, 2001).

Note: I have not included a table of Bloom's psychomotor domain as this work remained unfinished. It progresses from *perception* or *imitation* through *manipulation* and *precision* up to something like *articulation* or *adaptation* and *naturalisation*, but is less developed than the other domains.

A related, but different kind of taxonomy was created by Morgan and Saxton in 1987, focusing on personal engagement. They recognise that emotional engagement is more difficult to judge than cognitive and physical tasks since the latter can be measured and observed. To help teachers gauge the engagement of their pupils, they compiled the taxonomy presented in Table 4.4.

Through careful and appropriate questioning, cognitive challenge can be incorporated into lessons, regardless of subject matter and available resources.

How useful are thinking skills strategies and philosophy with children?

On the DCSF Standards website (www.standards.dcsf.gov.uk) there is an extensive area devoted to thinking skills, which has been necessary since these are now explicitly included in the National Curriculum. They acknowledge that 'it is difficult to get information about the range of programmes that are available, particularly from a teacher's perspective' and then go on to provide further information. They provide a taxonomy of different skills such as 'information-processing', 'enquiry', 'creative thinking', 'evaluation' and 'reasoning' as well as explaining three main approaches: philosophical approaches, brain-based learning and cognitive intervention approaches.

Brain-based learning approaches have been discussed in the popular press as well as in academic journals and include the work of practitioners such as de Bono and Gardner as well as theories or movements such as Neuro-Linguistic Programming (NLP), Accelerated Learning and Brain Gym (see the TLRP report, 2007 for a summary of the latest research). Despite these ideas being advertised as useful for highly able children, none of the schools we visited hold them up as a solution for keeping the able engaged. Some of the techniques and strategies are undoubtedly useful, but should be treated with caution and never viewed as a panacea.

Cognitive interventions incorporate the work of psychologists to improve thinking and the published programmes have been empirically tested over the years with mixed reviews. As with many pedagogies, fans of the techniques enthuse over them while others are sceptical. The efficacy of the strategies depends to a large extent on the commitment of the practitioner and the support of the management structures.

Evidence for the efficacy of some strategies is limited. Consider the following: How important is it for you to only use strategies that have been tried and tested? Does it matter if a technique works well, but is founded on

Table 4.4 Taxonomy of personal engagement (most advanced at bottom of table)

Level of involvement	How engaged pupils behave	Questions to help planning
Interest: being curious about what is presented	Make and maintain eye contact; listen; respond (verbal and non-verbal responses).	What questions shall I ask to attract attention?
Engaging: wanting to be involved in the task	Participate; follow instructions; adhere to classroom rules; work independently (alone or with others).	What shall I ask that will let their ideas be an important part of the process?
Committing: developing a sense of responsibility towards the task	Absorbed in tasks; confidence to manage the work and control its direction and development.	What questions will help them take responsibility in the enquiry?
Internalising: merging objective concepts (the task or what is to be learned) with subjective experience (what is already owned) resulting in understanding and ownership of new ideas	Moving from confusion to satisfaction, from mildly anxious activity to calm; establishing a clear connection to material already known; facial expression and posture can indicate this shift, as well as obvious reporting from pupils – 'I've got it!'	What questions will create an environment that encourages the reflection of thoughts, feelings, viewpoints, experiences and values?
Interpreting: wanting and needing to communicate that understanding to others	Wanting to talk about work, hearing from others and sharing or defending their views; keen to make predictions and suggest further possibilities.	What questions will invite pupils' expression of their understanding of the world and to help formulate new questions arising from their understanding?
Evaluating: wanting and being willing to put new understanding to the test	Pupils test out their understanding on a wider audience (such as parents); introducing their ideas in different contexts.	What shall I ask to allow them to test their new thinking in different media?

Note: adapted from Morgan and Saxton, 2006: 28–33.

questionable theory? Do you think that strategies can only be considered as effective if they work in a range of different contexts?

Philosophy with/for Children (P4C also PwC/PfC)

In recent years, the idea of using philosophy to challenge able pupils has spread quietly through many schools and colleges in the UK. Some specific qualities of P4C make it particularly useful in providing challenge to the highly able child. The growth of philosophy can be summarised through the figures presented by the International Council of Philosophical Inquiry with Children (ICPIC) and the European Foundation for the Advancement of Doing Philosophy with Children (SOPHIA). Both organisations report an increase in interest and queries. Through the growth of philosophy with children, there has been commensurate expansion of methods and pedagogies.

Researching approaches to children teaching and learning philosophy will likely throw up distinctions between Philosophy for Children (P4C/PfC), Philosophy with Children (PwC), or the Community of Philosophical Inquiry method (CoPI). Whilst differences exist (see McCall, 2007, for a relevant discussion of these), what is more marked is the similar aim of challenging pupils of all abilities through a dialogic approach.

Despite a growth in the incidence of philosophy in schools, comparatively few schools offer any kind of formal or informal philosophy opportunities for their pupils. Where such practice exists, incidence is erratic, approaches vary and the continuation of the work often depends heavily on the enthusiasm and dedication of a few individuals. The subject remains a low priority lacking resources and expertise. (For a full discussion of the role and development of philosophy in schools see Hand and Winstanley, 2007.)

So, what's different about philosophy when it comes to improving thinking? Philosophy is synonymous with critical thinking. The focus of the subject is the development of propensities and abilities to adopt a philosophical attitude, not just the understanding of philosophical ideas and knowledge of key texts in the canon. Children are required to assess reason against clear standards.

Many of the thinking skills programmes affix 'metacognitive' activities to existing subject areas, but in philosophy, this is already a key part of the task, since what is being developed is high-quality argument. Whilst other thinking skills programmes and other curriculum subjects might incorporate critical thinking, it will *always* be central to philosophy.

Unlike thinking skills programmes (of whatever type), philosophy is an academic discipline in its own right. Some thinking skills programmes use subject areas as their vehicle, but they are applying the topic to the skills, or applying the skills to the topic as a kind of infusion. This is quite different from the subject being critical thinking, which is the case in philosophy.

Practitioners of P4C recommend an *inductive* approach to working in philosophy. They consider it preferable to teach pupils (especially younger pupils) to 'do philosophy' rather than 'study philosophy'. This is a focus on philosophic enquiry and dialogue. All approaches require the creation of a Community of Enquiry (CoE), which is a collaborative, reflective discussion, sometimes described as 'thinking with one big head' (Kessels, 1997, cited in Murris, 2000). The CoE is optimally built up over time, with the same group of learners and the objectives are to create a community that cooperates and cares. It should be based on mutual respect and provide a safe space for the expression of ideas in the group search for understanding, meaning and values, always supported by reasons.

Box 4.5 provides a list of the central tenets of P4C. How effective are you with regard to the following principles?

Box 4.5 Central tenets of P4C

- Encouraging questioning and discriminating between assumptions, facts and judgements.
- Promoting dialogue through sitting in a circle and allowing pupils to lead and direct their own discussion, with you barely contributing verbally;
- Encouraging useful argument through fostering impersonal disagreement and modelling logical lines of reasoning.
- Developing abstract concepts through pointing out connections and promoting breadth and depth as appropriate (and providing ample time).
- Requiring logic and reason by identifying fallacies and spurious facts and by drawing attention to rationality.

Independent project work

Allowing pupils to engage in work that they direct and organise themselves is a sure-fire way to keep them motivated and on task. The advantages parallel the differences between deep and surface learning, where ownership and investment affect commitment and eventual outcome. (See Chapter 5 for further detail of pupils as researchers.)

Contemplate Table 4.5 relating the definitions to your own experience of learning (particularly at school, college or university) as well as the attitudes of the pupils with whom you work.

Independent learning is encouraged in the case-study schools through the use of 'Individual Challenge Plans' (ICPs), outlining an individual pupil's provision, for a either a project, a half-term, a term or the entire academic

Table 4.5 Surface and deep learning

Surface learning	Deep learning
Uncritical acceptance of new ideas	Critical analysis of new ideas
Confusing points of view with evidence	Distinguishing between fact and opinion
Lack of connections to knowledge or other subjects	Linking new ideas to existing knowledge and other subjects
Rote learning	Focus on meaning
Tasks undertaken for external reward and viewed as discrete	Tasks viewed as part of overall development
No attention paid to the substance or structure of the topic	Interested in content and structure of subject
Covering lots of material scantily	Focusing on key ideas in depth
Letting assessment lead working practices	Making assessment a vital part of learning

year. They may incorporate extra-curricular activities or specialist services and are created as a result of pupils negotiating with their teachers. Parents or other community members are involved if appropriate.

Many straightforward photocopiable template project planners are readily available and these can be helpful for shorter and simpler projects. More detailed and well-honed planners are recommended for longer-term work, and if the pupils are going to decrease their reliance on adult support, these are required.

The next section considers the TASC Framework as one means of developing independent and personalised learning across the curriculum.

TASC: thinking actively in a social context

The principles underlying the TASC Framework derive mainly from the work of three writers and researchers:

- *Vygotsky* argues that learning takes place when learners and mentors negotiate meaning, with the learners extending their understanding into new areas of competence and knowing. Vygotsky also emphasises that learners are enabled to learn when they can identify with the context and see the relevance of their learning. He sees the development of language and thinking as symbiotic key elements. Hence the overall importance of language, mediation and negotiation of understanding.
- *Sternberg* stresses that 'intelligence' is fundamentally problem-solving and *all* learners can improve their capacities to solve problems when they acquire a wide range of skills and strategies which are learned through active engagement with relevant problem-solving activities. Sternberg

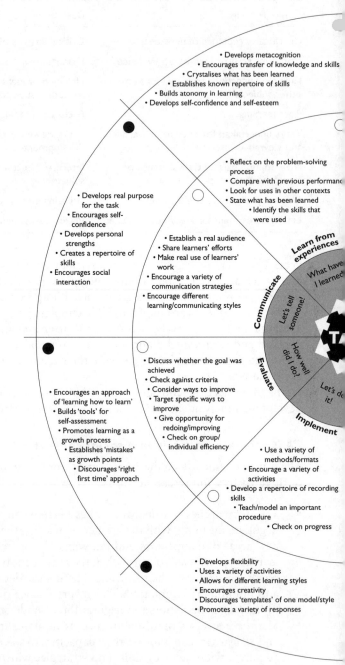

Figure 4.2 The TASC Problem-solving Wheel

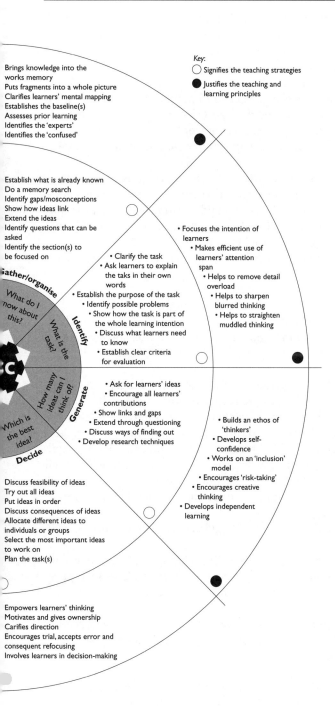

Brings knowledge into the
works memory
Puts fragments into a whole picture
Clarifies learners' mental mapping
Establishes the baseline(s)
Assesses prior learning
Identifies the 'experts'
Identifies the 'confused'

Key:
○ Signifies the teaching strategies
● Justifies the teaching and
learning principles

Establish what is already known
Do a memory search
Identify gaps/mosconceptions
Show how ideas link
Extend the ideas
Identify questions that can be
asked
Identify the section(s) to
be focused on

Gather/organise
What do I
now about
this?

What is the
task?

Identify

How many
ideas can I
think of?

Generate

Which is
the best
idea?

Decide

• Clarify the task
• Ask learners to explain
  the taks in their own
  words
• Establish the purpose of the task
• Identify possible problems
• Show how the task is part of
  the whole learning intention
• Discuss what learners need
  to know
• Establish clear criteria
  for evaluation

• Ask for learners' ideas
• Encourage all learners'
  contributions
• Show links and gaps
• Extend through questioning
• Discuss ways of finding out
• Develop research techniques

• Focuses the intention of
  learners
• Makes efficient use of
  learners' attention
  span
• Helps to remove detail
  overload
• Helps to sharpen
  blurred thinking
• Helps to straighten
  muddled thinking

• Builds an ethos of
  'thinkers'
• Develops self-
  confidence
• Works on an 'inclusion'
  model
• Encourages 'risk-taking'
• Encourages creative
  thinking
• Develops independent
  learning

Discuss feasibility of ideas
Try out all ideas
Put ideas in order
Discuss consequences of ideas
Allocate different ideas to
individuals or groups
Select the most important ideas
to work on
Plan the task(s)

Empowers learners' thinking
Motivates and gives ownership
Carifies direction
Encourages trial, accepts error and
consequent refocusing
Involves learners in decision-making

also maintains that problem-solving is both analytic and creative, with a strong practical component. Hence 'intelligence' is not a static state that can be 'measured' with a 'one-off score' but is a dynamic concept that develops through active problem-solving processing.

- *Bandura* maintains that effective teaching and learning relies on the affective relationship between teachers and pupils – teachers conveying a sense of belief in pupils' capacities and learners perceiving that belief in their efficacy. Moreover, learning is not only an individual journey, but is socially constructed through group interaction (Wallace, 2004).

In addition, the development of the TASC Framework is derived from Living Theory in which facilitators and learners are actively engaged in evolving the theory and practice of learning and teaching using the principles outlined above (see Wallace, 2008 for a full account of the theory, development and practice of the TASC Framework).

Belle Wallace's TASC Framework is fully outlined in Figure 4.2. The figure explains:

- The stages of the TASC Problem-solving Framework;
- The teaching strategies that bring about ownership and personalised learning and that enable independent thinking and decision-making;
- The teaching and learning principles that underpin TASC.

The TASC Framework outlines the stages of expert thinking: all the TASC stages are important, but the stages are recursive and flexible, allowing the learner to review and reflect, to rethink their thinking and make changes. *All learners can think* and so, importantly, TASC is inclusive; more able pupils are well able to use the TASC Framework independently, whilst pupils needing more support can use the Framework as scaffolding for their thinking. TASC is used extensively across schools in the UK as a Framework that allows personalised learning, giving learners ownership and opportunities for decision-making.

A systematic review of thinking skills (Higgins *et al.*, 2004) reported that:

> TASC appears positively to promote the development of cognitive skills and strategies. Self-monitoring and reflection enables students to improve their solutions and to become more effective thinkers.

A more recent case-study review carried out across 4,000 classrooms systematically using TASC (Wallace, 2008) yielded the following comments from teachers and pupils:

- *Motivation, independence and engagement* – overwhelmingly, the teachers reported that pupils' motivation and engagement with the learning tasks were increased to the point where they hardly needed to intervene in the learning activity. The TASC Framework supplied the structure which all children were keen to engage with, and the teacher's role became that of a facilitator rather than an instructor.

> Children who are never engaged with learning and who generally need constant supervision just got on with the task they had decided on. They were making their own decisions, I realised it was because they had ownership.

- *Self-esteem, enjoyment and success* – there was general consensus that the children enjoyed their work and entered fully into the thinking processes and the celebration of their success.

> A child who is normally the 'outsider' was an accepted member of the group. I realised that he is an excellent practical problem-solver and when the group praised his work, he just beamed!

- *Diminished antisocial behaviour and increased socially acceptable behaviour* – there was unanimous agreement that there had been positive change in pupils' emotional and social behaviour.

> My class is a very challenging class and I was sceptical that working in the TASC way would make any difference. But I was amazed at what the children already knew and how excited they were because they could choose which questions they wanted to explore. I really was surprised that they could work without arguing and shouting!

Amongst the general comments expressed by teachers the following is typical:

> Our very able children on the 'gifted' Register [for language and mathematics] have exceeded all our expectations. We realised that they were just coasting. We have been amazed at what they have been able to do! But we have extended our concept of 'more able' and now we celebrate every child.

And the pupils were quite capable of recognising their own growth and excitement:

> I realised that TASC is already in my head but I didn't know it! I use the TASC Wheel to guide my thinking.
>
> TASC days 'confidences us up' so we are not afraid to speak out in front of other people.
>
> TASC gives us a full packed education! We didn't realise until afterwards that we had done research, history, ICT [Information and Communication Technology], art, craft, DT [Design Technology], drama, speaking and listening. We even did some Literacy and we enjoyed it!
>
> TASC days are exciting because 'you can open up your creative side'. Teachers don't say that's wrong and it takes a lot of pressure off you.

For further details of the TASC Framework, see www.tascwheel.com and www.nace.co.uk.

Conclusion to Part 2

It would be misleading for me to suggest that the techniques discussed here are always easy to implement. Ensuring cognitive challenge, improving questioning, developing thinking, fostering philosophical dispositions and allowing plenty of independent project work will always need a skilled practitioner if they are to really challenge pupils. They are all feasible and effective strategies and those who have made them work often started out with only minimal help and support. The hope is that as practice is examined and understood, practitioners will have an easier time getting to grips with these excellent ways of embedding challenge in their classrooms.

Overall conclusion

Rather than summarising what has gone before, I have provided mini-conclusions for Part 1 and Part 2. I will end here with a quotation from Holt's seminal text *How Children Fail*, first published in 1964. He writes here about the notion of curiosity. Since this is what challenge is designed to pique, it is an apt point on which to finish:

> Curiosity is hardly ever idle. What we want to know, we want to know for a reason. The reason is that there is a hole, a gap, an empty space in our understanding of things, our mental model of the world. . . . when the gap is filled, we feel pleasure, satisfaction, relief.
>
> (1982: 87–8)

All pupils thrive on well-conceived challenge. Able, gifted and talented learners need equal challenge to their peers in order to participate in schooling, express their abilities and aim for excellence.

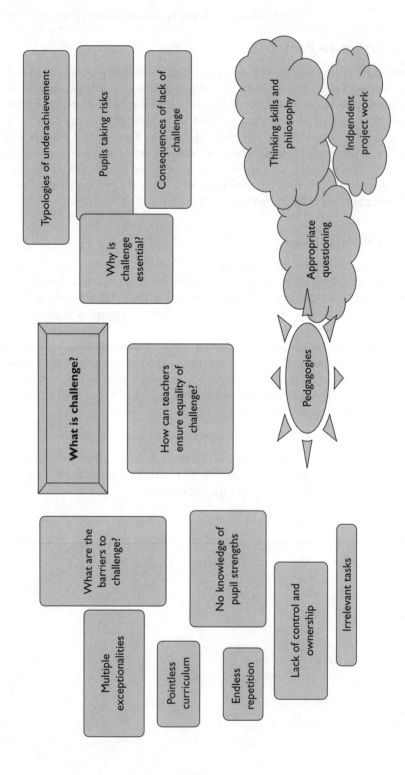

Figure 4.3 Summary concept map 4

References and further reading

DCSF 'Thinking skills in primary classrooms'. Online: www.standards.dfes. gov.uk/thinkingskills/ (accessed 5 February 2009).

European Foundation for the Advancement of Doing Philosophy with Children (SOPHIA). Online: http://sophia.eu.org/ (accessed 5 February 2009).

Freeman, J. (1997) 'The emotional development of the highly able', *European Journal of Psychology in Education*, 12: 479–493.

Griffin, N. S. and McKenzie, J. (1992) *Nebraska Starry Night: Observation Protocol, a Behaviour-Based Early Identification Instrument*. Lincoln, NE: University of Nebraska-Lincoln.

Hand, M. and Winstanley, C. (eds) (2007) *Philosophy in Schools*. London: Continuum.

Higgins, S., Baumfield, V., Lin, M., Moseley, D., Butterworth, M., Downey, G., Gregson, M., Oberski, I., Rockett, M. and Thacker, D. (2004) 'Thinking skills approaches to effective teaching and learning: what is the evidence for impact on learners'. In *Research Evidence in Education Library*, London: EPPI-Centre (Social Science Research Unit, Institute of Education).

Holt, J. (1964, 1982) *How Children Fail*. London: Delta.

International Council of Philosophical Inquiry with Children (ICPIC). Online: www.icpic.org/ (accessed 5 February 2009).

McCall, C. (2007) 'Philosophical inquiry and lifelong learning: life, the universe and everything', *Proceedings of the International Conference on Dialogue, Culture and Philosophy*, Graz, 2006, Sankt Augustin: Academia Verlag.

Montgomery, D. (2000) *Able Underachievers*. London: Whurr Publishers.

Morgan, N. and Saxton, J. (2006) *Asking Better Questions*. Markham, Ontario: Pembroke Publishers.

Murris, K. (2000) 'Can children do philosophy?', *Journal of Philosophy of Education*, 34 (2): 261–279.

Van Tassel-Baska, J. (2004) 'Quo Vadis? Laboring in the classical vineyards: an optimal challenge for gifted secondary students', *Journal of Secondary Gifted Education*, 15 (2): 56–60.

Wallace, B. (ed.) (2008) *Gifted Education International*, 24 (2 and 3). Oxford: AB Academic Publishers.

Wallace, B. (2002) *Teaching Thinking Skills Across the Middle Years*. London: David Fulton Publishers (A NACE-Fulton Pub.).

Wallace, B., Maker, J. and Cave. D. (2004) *Thinking Skills and Problem-Solving: An Inclusive Approach*. London: David Fulton Publishers (A NACE-Fulton Pub.).

Wallace, B., Fitton, S. Leyden, S., Montgomery, D., Pomerantz, M. and Winstanley, C. (2007) *Raising the Achievement of Able, Gifted and Talented Pupils within an Inclusive School Framework: Guidelines for Schools to Audit and Extend Existing Best Practice*. Oxford: National Association for Able Children in Education. publications@nace.co.uk.

Winstanley, C. (forthcoming) *The Ingredients of Challenge*. Staffs: Stoke on Trent Trentham Books.

Winstanley, C. (2004) *Too Clever by Half: a fair deal for gifted children*. Staffs: Stoke on Trent Trentham Books.

References for tables

Anderson, L. W. and Krathwohl, D. R. (eds) (2001). *A Taxonomy for Learning, Teaching and Assessing: a Revision of Bloom's Taxonomy of Educational Objectives*. New York: Longman.

Anderson, L.W. and Sosniak, L. A. (eds) (1994). *Bloom's Taxonomy: a Forty-year Retrospective*. Ninety-third yearbook of the National Society for the Study of Education, Pt. 2. Chicago: University of Chicago Press.

Bloom, B. S. (1956) *Taxonomy of Educational Objectives, Handbook I: The Cognitive Domain*. New York: David McKay Co., Inc.

Clark, D. (no date) Online: www.nwlink.com/~donclark/hrd/bloom.html (accessed 17 March 2005).

Dave, R. H. (1975). *Developing and Writing Behavioural Objectives*. Ed. R. J. Armstrong. Educational Innovators Press.

Eisner, E. W. (2002) *Benjamin Bloom 1913–99*. International Bureau of Education: UNESCO. Online: www.ibe.unesco.org/International/Publications/Thinkers/ThinkersPdf/bloome.pdf (accessed 31 March 2005).

Harrow, A. (1972) *A Taxonomy of Psychomotor Domain: a Guide for Developing Behavioural Objectives*. New York: David McKay.

Krathwohl, D. R. (2002). 'A revision of bloom's taxonomy: an overview', *Theory into Practice*, 41 (4): 212–218.

Krathwohl, D. R., Bloom, B. S. and Bertram, B. M. (1973) *Taxonomy of Educational Objectives, the Classification of Educational Goals. Handbook II: Affective Domain*. New York: David McKay Co., Inc.

Powell, R., McIntyre, E. and Rightmeyer, E. (2006) 'Johnny won't read, and Susie won't either: reading instruction and student resistance', *Journal of Early Childhood Literacy*, 6 (1): 5–31.

Simpson, E. J. (1972) *The Classification of Educational Objectives in the Psychomotor Domain*. Washington: Gryphon House.

TLRP (2007) *Neuroscience and Education: Issues and Opportunities. A Commentary by the Teaching Learning and Research Programme*. London: TLRP. Online: www.tlrp.org/pub/documents/Neuroscience%20Commentary%20FINAL.pdf.

Chapter 5

Defining a research community

Michael Pomerantz

Introduction

The following chapter aspires to demonstrate convincingly that a carefully assembled group of gifted and talented (G + T) pupils collectively called a research community or RC could help to solve many complicated and serious social problems facing individuals and schools. At the same time this RC would address the participants' strong need to express themselves far more creatively than applies at present in many schools where their obvious skills and potential contributions are underutilised. There is a history to this but we will leave that particular investigation to educational historians and sociologists. We see pupils endowed with enormous assets who could offer so much more to their schools if they were given the proper opportunity. They could promote social justice, reduce marginalisation, encourage participatory citizenship and reduce waste of time and effort. They could effectively harness and utilise the energy of pupils that is often diverted into antisocial behaviour that can substantially reduce what is learned in school.

What do we mean by a research community?

It might be helpful initially to perceive RCs rather flexibly as anything from a simple dialogue involving a pupil and a teacher communicating about some research to a more formally composed research group. This chapter will address the notion of community, RC attributes, membership, commissioning, doing research and solving problems. Then we will focus on four innovative and exemplary schools which have independently engaged in activities that are very much within the spirit of a RC.

Some adults are fascinated with what is happening within normal school-based conversation or discourse, while others are particularly attracted to what we are not talking about or what we are selectively avoiding. Some of this we do consciously while some of this is done unconsciously. This chapter asks that we examine a rather obvious, simple and highly cost effective RC solution to what needs to be improved in schools, utilising pupils in a manner that we have underutilised for far too long and at too great a cost. It builds upon the substantial social price some pay for tolerating the old notion that 'children are meant to be seen and not heard'. The richness of the basic discourse between teachers and students should be a hallmark of a RC.

Most adults would probably feel the above saying is rather dated but we could ask ourselves if we collectively are really listening to all of what is being said. Are we really sufficiently curious about the substantial views of our students and how could we persuasively show this with some solid evidence? If an Ofsted inspector asked to see evidence of the real impact of our listening to the voices of children, an obvious and convincing response would be to highlight the influence of what the RC has done for the fabric of the overall school community. We are not speaking of simple political rhetoric here but of measurable and substantial evidence that can be seen. A proper RC should be prepared to take a deep look at the status quo, the various comfort zones and how some vested interests are blocking substantial change and improvement. Its intent is not subversive but simply to uncover what is not surfacing on the public agenda with any great clarity or salience.

What are some origins and attributes of research communities?

This developing work has a precedent and it derives from liberal and emancipatory traditions as seen within the writings of Paulo Freire, A. S. Neill and Carl Rogers. For too long, we have tended to relegate liberal thought to what were perceived as failed experiments in education in the last century. There were admittedly educational advocates who tended to want pupils to read and write for pleasure and to extract the meaning of text without sufficient care given to more traditional emphasis placed upon structure, discipline and grammar. With the arrival of the prescriptive National Curriculum, the setting of numerous targets for students and staff alike, and top-down impositions we have lost something of education being a simple encounter between the teacher and the pupil. The RC working with and for school staff can redress some of this loss.

The proposed RC has essential attributes that constitute its identity while allowing great imagination and scope in creating a social organisation that is actually fit for purpose and feels like an entity created within, and conspicuously owned by, a wider host-school community. We will start with the core or essential attributes of this special community:

- The RC should ideally be initiated with a small group of school pupils that either formulates itself, perhaps at the inspiration of one or two keen individual students, or it is invited to gather together by staff such as the G + T coordinator or the headteacher (HT).
- All participants are volunteers. Ideally, the initial group should consist of a suitable cross section of male and female G + T pupils from different

year groups. Within the first year, they will probably devise the sensible membership rules so as to create a working unit that is their own creation, rather than one orchestrated by adult staff. If attenders do not feel they possess the creativity and the responsible autonomy to complete their tasks, momentum and volunteering may be lost. Rigorously supporting these evolutionary principles is one important activity that staff can contribute.

• RCs could self-volunteer for activities that are broadly grouped into categories; for example, political affairs, environmental issues, ethics of scientific research, and so on as well as school concerns such as under-achievement, bullying or truancy.

In time the RC will devise its own name, its own purpose, which may change over time, and the constituent group membership. It will seek to find its unique social position within the overall school system and over time it will develop its own traditions, its own language and its own history. The RC will meet at times and within venues best chosen for convenience, productivity and efficiency with staff support from the start.

This chapter describes a series of very real proposals that can be presented as a concept to others including the staff, the parents, the governors, etc. Some of the ideas presented have been piloted already in schools but others are awaiting exploration and exploitation by readers and their colleagues and, hopefully, by some secondary-aged pupils themselves. Pupils will begin to tell this story themselves in various formats including conference presentations and film making. The evolution of RCs in schools might allow staff to deal with systemic solutions to long-term school problems that have historically proven highly resistant to interventions that do not address systems per se but are mainly targeted at individuals.

Figure 5.1 summarises the attributes of a research community.

What might constitute core RC membership and recruitment?

The RC might be composed of representative pupils from Years 7 to 13, or the age range might be extended or made narrower for some reason. The RC might remain a small functional unit, or expand with subcommittees dealing with different functions and tasks. Its organisation would be hopefully democratic and it would publish whatever statement of its structure, its procedures, its rules of operations and its values that its members decide, assuming essential Senior Management Team (SMT) support. Too much inspirational and organisational shaping by well intended adult professionals is counter-indicated for reasons that should become obvious in the lines that follow. More can be expected from a group that feels it can pilot its own journey.

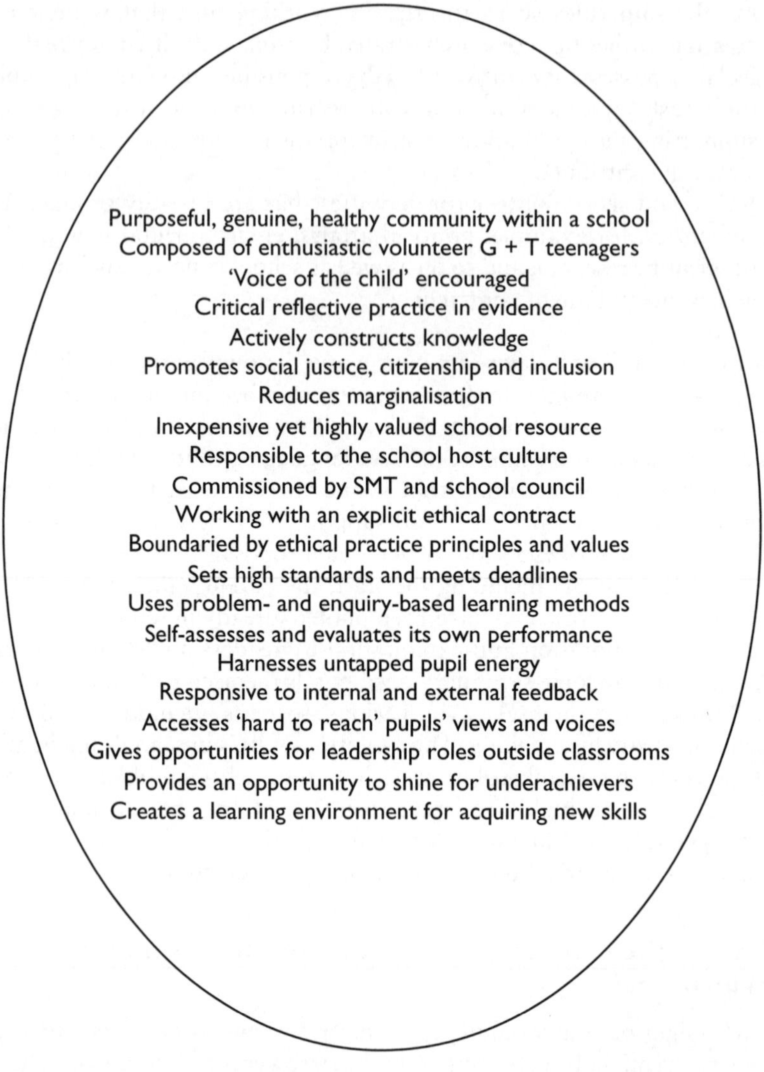

Purposeful, genuine, healthy community within a school
Composed of enthusiastic volunteer G + T teenagers
'Voice of the child' encouraged
Critical reflective practice in evidence
Actively constructs knowledge
Promotes social justice, citizenship and inclusion
Reduces marginalisation
Inexpensive yet highly valued school resource
Responsible to the school host culture
Commissioned by SMT and school council
Working with an explicit ethical contract
Boundaried by ethical practice principles and values
Sets high standards and meets deadlines
Uses problem- and enquiry-based learning methods
Self-assesses and evaluates its own performance
Harnesses untapped pupil energy
Responsive to internal and external feedback
Accesses 'hard to reach' pupils' views and voices
Gives opportunities for leadership roles outside classrooms
Provides an opportunity to shine for underachievers
Creates a learning environment for acquiring new skills

Figure 5.1 Attributes of a research community

The question of why we start with G + T pupils has been legitimately asked by professionals who promote inclusive practice and who wonder if the G + T cohort are being given special privileges and a status not allowed to the vast majority of other school pupils. This is an understandable question and hopefully the following response is appropriately reasonable. For example, any school could adopt a policy to recruit students to its student council or youth forum. This already happens, showing the wider community that the SMT is interested in working with and hearing the 'voice of the child'. These pupils are nominated and selected by a process that particularly values leadership and citizenship skills, and those chosen are often considered popular and best placed to speak for the majority. Elected members should represent a broad political base. The composition of these groups is not challenged as non-inclusive or as discriminating against those who are less well liked at school. It is considered important that student council or forum members are selected in an open, accountable and public electoral process and that those chosen are deemed to be best placed to do this given organisational task. The student government group is not established by means of a random selection lottery. Those actually chosen for sports teams or for musical groups are likely to demonstrate strong potential in these areas.

The new proposed RC serves another function in that it offers the school community a specialist team of G + T pupils who bring unique critical and reflective research skills to bear upon problems that can and do baffle adults. It allows participants to make a substantial contribution that is both highly desirable and not currently happening in many schools today, although some embryonic RC activities are acknowledged. In most cases the RC should not redundantly constitute a group that is already in operation. It should be a noticeable addition for a school and something which would serve the school well as a value-added resource. Without the initial G + T uniqueness of the group composition, the RC would be starting off with far less research output potential. Over time, it is highly likely that the group composition will widen as members will want their friends who are not all G + T to be drafted onboard as additional recruits. This is both predictable and natural and should not reduce overall potential output. The RC should have control over who joins them and how new recruits are located and selected including self-nomination by enthusiastic volunteers.

The RC should not be interpreted as elitist but more as a form of practical meritocracy. Schools should value the contributions that RC members bestow freely upon the school. The powers of the RC would be limited to supporting and informing the SMT and others such as the student council. The RC would not be seeking to establish a political base but would serve to provide evidence-based, informed views on topics of concern to the wider school. What is actually done with the output of the RC is very much in the hands of those who commission the research such as the SMT and the student council.

How might the commissioning and contracting processes operate?

Commissioning of its research activities is another essential and defining attribute of the proposed RCs. Without a commission, productivity is likely to stall at the first hurdle. If there are a number of RC subgroups in a school, then the focus of each can be different according to their interests. In most instances the RC would meet on a few occasions for initial team-building and consolidation exercises, to allow its identity to be partially formulated primarily based upon the motivations and the specific interests of the initial G + T participants. The RC might meet alone without any adult support in the room, or its earliest operations might be facilitated by the presence of a staff member (perhaps the G + T coordinator, or a teacher particularly interested in research per se.) Once the RC has a clear idea of what it wants to research, its spokesperson (perhaps its leader or the chair or a member with ambassadorial skills) would formally approach commissioners. From this point forward reference will be made to the HT as one commissioner, although in practice RC liaison might take place with any representative of the SMT. Some RCs might seek tutorial support and expertise from staff on specific research problems, but other RCs might prefer to adopt a problem- or enquiry-based approach within which members would have to look for answers themselves, possibly without the benefit of much formal training in how to do research. Box 5.1 summarises some of the questions the SMT might ask.

Box 5.1   Possible initial questions posed by the SMT

- What does the RC want to research?
- How it will demonstrate its research competence?
- What different methodologies will be employed?
- How it will time manage its projects?
- What potential risks are involved?
- How are research ethics being addressed?
- How the RC might create problems for the school?
- Who will own the collected data?
- How will the output be disseminated?

The HT will probably seek, and will need to gain reassurances, that the research is ethical and boundaried by a written contract, or a verbally agreed contract between the SMT and the RC. Once commissioned, the RC would be conspicuously identified as a group acting with the consent and approval of the SMT. The RC would not be disadvantaged or marginalised by members having to prove themselves to others such as school administrators or the teachers responsible for the timetable or room allocations whose cooperation and assistance might be invaluable. The RC would hold a published mandate. Their output would ideally be recognised and valued.

The RC will not be given an unlimited hunting licence to probe into any area of school business and then selectively write and edit whatever output it so desires. The contract would specify any project parameters and the ownership of what is found and publicised. It is assumed that, in the beginning, the RC would be commissioned to undertake smaller and perhaps safer tasks or projects and that successful contractual completion would be publicly rewarded with a future and perhaps more substantial contract, extending work onto larger and possibly more challenging topics. To keep the motivation of the RC intact, members would need clear reassurances that their research output would be respected, and some would lead to noticeable and acknowledged school improvement. In that way everyone benefits. RC members would hopefully be rewarded with some imaginative credit for their substantial voluntary research which might be interpreted as extra-curricular, but which ought to be seamlessly integrated within normal school work. Their teachers in particular ought to see and acknowledge how the research activity is helping with education generally and within the wider curriculum in particular. RC members with aspirations to attend university should find the investigatory work uplifting, and it should provide the foundations for more independent and rigorous study as they become older. They would have had substantially more 'hands-on' experience with research than would otherwise have been the case.

How might research be conducted?

The RC is one way to prioritise school improvement and to show this as a purposeful and honourable activity for students and not just staff. The RC could make a difference to any school. The skills being developed by its members would include the elements in Box 5.2.

Box 5.2 Skills being developed by the RC

- Research planning
- Methodology selection
- Ethical considerations
- Enquiry and hypothesis formulation
- Use of information technology
- Data gathering, data analysis and interpretation, validation
- Formulation of conclusions, report writing and presentation.

Another essential attribute of the RC is the priority placed upon knowledge construction, in marked contrast to a chronic overemphasis on knowledge dissemination, which already plays too big a role in many schools today. Evidence stemming from work within previous and existing RCs repeatedly tells us the familiar story of able students who are not really working towards their potential and who report that they are often seriously bored with school. This then leads towards underachievement which, if chronic, costs both the pupil and the school. It can become another lost opportunity.

A student-led RC might elect to seek out specifically the voices of those defined as 'hard to reach' who might be seen as non-conformists or marginalised. Opinion polls often do not tap into the sources of those who might have the most to tell us in our efforts to solve complex adolescent problems. The RC would have to dig deeper into the methodological problems of how to listen and how to hear those whose messages are most important to our queries. There are often great and profound social insights amongst those who are currently perceived as angry, vulnerable, unattached or withdrawn at school. The RC would be charged with encouraging conversations that are not currently occurring, with enough salience to make much difference to school improvement.

The RC would have access to a wide range of research activity and methods that would not be limited to simplistic surveys, and members would be able to choose between quantitative and qualitative approaches depending on what they are seeking to discover. There are interesting developments involving new technology such as interactive websites with voting procedures, video diary booths, video observations in school settings and various types of texting using both computers and mobile technologies. For example, film making has become a far more dynamic way to publish research findings for a diverse audience than the more traditional procedure of writing an academic paper for a limited audience.

How might students be able to study and even help to solve problems that baffle adults?

Another defining attribute of a really productive RC is that the focus of research should be something that directly appeals to the members' personal interests while simultaneously having the qualities that are likely to earn them a commission from the SMT. Too much steerage or influence from adults can kill off spontaneity and enthusiasm which are the engines that drive research commitment. While it might be preferable for a new RC to embark on a modest project with a high probability of a successful outcome, that choice needs to be taken by the RC participants themselves. Taking on too big a task might compromise the RC from the start.

The evolution of a RC or multiple RCs in a single school offers a much needed and new positive sense of optimism at a time when the public are growing very tired of overly familiar, pessimistic, political rhetoric that sounds like 'never again'. This was heard after World War I when people hoped that never again would we be faced with a similar global war situation. It was heard after the 1999 Sir William MacPherson Inquiry into the death of Stephen Lawrence and more recently with the Victoria Climbie Inquiry. When something tragic happens at a national level there is a noted tendency to allocate responsibility on a formal basis to professionals to look into what lessons can be learned so fresh legislation and new guidance can be issued. This simplistic resolution rarely achieves its promise. In 2009, the newspaper and broadcasting media are asking searching questions about the apparent increase in antisocial behaviour, such as bullying, and challenges that lead towards exclusions. An extreme example might be to look at students possessing and using knives in school settings, in stark contrast from the standard perspective of adults examining a threatening problem. It could be speculated that whatever gets published about knife possession will be predictable and might not lower our fears about knives being carried into schools. Students doing research into any form of antisocial behaviour are likely to come to different conclusions from those produced by adults. It is not advocated that a new RC undertake such a large and sensitive project but we could not rule out the contribution RCs could make to our overall understanding of knife possession.

A RC within a particular school just might be more helpful in constructing the knowledge necessary to tackle any serious social justice and vulnerability issue than for the local adults working alone to sort this out themselves. The work of the RC could complement whatever well-intended activities are mounted by the staff and the wider community outside of school. The RC might ask who owns any particular problem? Is it a student issue that needs pupil investigation and resolution, or should the whole matter simply be left to the SMT and governors as applies with most traditional school based problems? The RC could be specifically commissioned to ask some really basic research questions, such as: Why do pupils violate the norms or rules of schools? Or, why does bullying seem to be on the increase despite all the well-intended interventions? They might help us better understand the practice of happy-slapping and the throwing of snowballs.

RCs can add to our understanding of teenage behaviour by focusing on any antisocial behaviour. Box 5.3 highlights possible questions with regard to an investigation of bullying.

Box 5.3 Possible questions with regard to an investigation about bullying

- What are the options and choices available to a pupil witnessing bullying?

- What motivates aggression?
- What is the difference between public behaviour and that which remains hidden or less visible?
- What do offenders gain by breaking school conventions?
- Is the school community aware of the essential descriptive statistics about the frequency, severity and duration of antisocial behaviour such as bullying?
- What antecedents precede bullying and what consequences follow it?
- Is the school community united in a campaign to reduce bullying or do opinions vary?
- What actually happens when bullying is seen in school by a bystander observer?
- How is bullying behaviour reported and is this effective? Why might it not be reported?
- Do students feel the current situation is hopeless, or might some combined staff and student action yield significant improvements?
- What has been the impact of previous staff attempts to reduce antisocial behaviour in this school? If the interventions fail, what lessons have been learned?
- Is there a school behaviour code and if so, who wrote it? Is it well known and appreciated?

When adults gather to solve problems, there is a tendency to look at the composition of any local or national inquiry panel to see that it is balanced and endowed with conspicuous competence and authority. There is always the risk that what is produced represents an echo chamber which simply resonates with the current establishment procedures and, therefore, produces little that is remarkably new and inspires pupils and staff with optimism about change. The proposed RC does not have that 'baggage' from its inception. Members hopefully are more inspired to find root causes and practical solutions than to prop up the status quo, particularly in cases where the current procedures to modify behaviour are not working effectively. Solutions can have a 'small is beautiful' character that builds upon local people and harnesses internal resources that are currently not being used to greatest effect. RCs are not necessarily dependent upon a strong and charismatic-type figure to lead people out of the wilderness. They work from a different base.

Figure 5.2 summarises the potential outcomes of a research community.

Noticeable school improvements
Raised aspirations and measured achievement
Improved pupil behaviour with fewer exclusions
Better understandings of pupil behaviour and interventions
Better engagement of 'hard to reach' pupils
Commissioned projects completed on schedule
Making a valued difference to the school community
Leaving an evidence trail of the work accomplished
Providing a fresh alternative perspective
Reports and films produced
Contributions for Ofsted and governors offered
New leadership skills gained for RC members and others
Wider ownership of school-based problems
New alliances with other schools' RCs
More optimism amongst staff
Raised morale and school cohesion
Peers can see positive whole school research outcomes
Teachers can see pupils in a completely different light
Sets precedent for student involvement in policies
Students from across KS3–5 work effectively
Students learn from each other

Figure 5.2 Outcomes of a research community

How can educational psychology contribute?

For many years, I have been involved as a trainer and as a manager of educational psychologists (EPs). Historically, EPs were asked to assess individual students looking primarily at problems such as limited intellectual potential, dyslexia or specific learning difficulties and emotional and/or behavioural challenges. Many EPs came to the conclusion that too much emphasis was being placed upon the individual and that EPs needed to step back and look at patterns such as the school's pastoral system, the inclusion and exclusions policies, curriculum delivery, staff training, staff development and staff support. Some EPs concluded that the best practice was to offer both individual casework to address the former issues with named pupils, while also offering consultancy for the latter issues primarily with staff, other professionals and parents.

This unique context has provided EPs with a privileged position to observe both what works and especially what does not work when it comes to targeting school improvement. Despite a vast array of professionals working both within and outside schools, we are now faced with major challenges in terms of socially unacceptable pupil conduct and record numbers of pupils being removed from school either on short fixed-term exclusions or permanently. One day, many of these previously excluded young people will become parents themselves, and when they come to enrol their own children in nursery and infant settings they may well arrive with angry and painful memories of their own last days in school and how they came to be rejected and excluded. Those memories may be accurate or otherwise, but the receiving HT may well face an uphill struggle establishing a positive relationship with a young adult carrying negative and counter-productive thoughts and feelings about past education. This is a time bomb that will confront the next generation of school leaders. One day, research will question the positive benefits of much exclusion.

Many children today are raised in Local Authority Care (LAC) and many are spending time in secure accommodation. Some pupils are considered violent. Some carry weapons into school. The fears experienced by adults are likely to stimulate reactive strategies such as installing metal detectors and 'zero tolerance' policies in schools. While these might prove very costly and marginally effective, they could simply mirror the procedure of installing expensive screening procedures at airports to deter terrorists. We can ask three vital questions:

- Do airline passengers feel safer today than they did twenty years ago?
- Are adults optimistic about how schools are dealing with their norm violators today?
- Would new approaches be valued?

Suppose that antisocial behaviour became a serious issue in a given school and that the RC was commissioned to study a particular problem and to offer suggestions for practical and affordable interventions. There is always the risk that pupils would be unable to recommend effective interventions, but the process of conducting the research would have been educational in itself, and presumably the SMT would have gained something from the RC's contribution. On a much more positive note, it is just possible that the RC would produce some realistic solutions to a very challenging social problem. The investment would have paid dividends, especially if the SMT was able to state its agreement with any intervention plans devised by the RC. Alternatively, the RC knowledge generation output might be just what the

SMT needs to create its own perhaps more comprehensive solutions. This would be a real partnership.

The RC might have adopted the notion that antisocial behaviour such as bullying in schools is not simply a staff problem, but a problem owned by the entire school community of adults and students. When a visitor sees teenagers throwing snowballs outside school, who owns that problem? This is where citizenship can be lifted from the pages of textbooks and transported into something visible and practical. Here problem ownership might have perceptually shifted and the reporting of unacceptable behaviour would have increased, as new suggestions are actually drafted by students. The relative positioning of young persons and adults outside an outdated 'cat and mouse' game may have shifted to everyone's benefit. We might see an alliance of adults coupled with the vast majority of the pupils who follow the rules, in opposition to a tiny minority who risk much by breaking school rules. The effect could well be emancipatory for the vast majority of normal pupils who simply want to continue peacefully with their education.

What is meant by a sense of community?

One of the great advantages of post-colonial thought is to be able to reflect at length on all that is lost when one culture or group feels itself to be vastly superior to another. By departing from the geographical territory of a former owner of colonies and by visiting an area such as the Caribbean, it is possible to see that a great legacy of colonial behaviour and deference that is still in evidence today. While slavery and indentured servitude may no longer be present, it is possible to witness a depressing tendency for some Caribbeans to look back to England for expertise, leadership and the setting of world-class standards when it comes to education. A more favourable post-modern alternative would be to ask what we in England can learn from the Caribbean. The example cited for this chapter is the notion of community. When a young child is born somewhere in St Lucia or Trinidad, that child is potentially more likely to feel himself or herself to be a part of a real community than a similar-aged counterpart in England.

While most pupils are members of families or extended families in both cultures, the pupil in England is probably less likely to feel himself or herself to be a valued member of what we mean by a community. Being a member of a community may offer a special heritage and some shared experiences, meanings, respect, rituals, vision, history, music and other traditions. One of the reasons that online Internet communities are so popular these days is that it fills a gap in the lives of many individuals.

The proposed RC here in this chapter is very much a self-sustaining and ideally thriving community of persons who gain something special by membership that is unavailable, or less likely to be found elsewhere. Some pupils do gain something of a sense of community by affiliating with a church, a mosque, the scouts or guides, although participation for many school-aged pupils is rather restricted by today's standards. The proposed RC would offer massive opportunities for G + T pupils that would otherwise not be readily available in school or elsewhere. Some G + T pupils have reported a sense of community by participating in the, now extinct, National Academy for Gifted and Talented Youth (NAGTY) activities.

What are some examples of RCs evolving?

The notion of a RC may appear novel to some readers, but examples of exemplary G + T research innovations involving pupils and staff collaborating will be cited from our case-study research. These examples show how some of the basic principles mentioned above can be seen to be evolving in four different secondary schools in England. In some cases it would be a simple task to reconceptualise and identify work already being undertaken as being, in essence, a RC in a hybrid fashion. For RCs to flourish and proliferate, it is important than their creative potential is not compromised by rigid definitions, unnecessary limitations or heavy external guidance on what might be created. (See Chapter 1 for a summary of the common characteristics shown by the twelve successful schools in the case study.)

Case studies

Fuller reports of successful practice in four secondary schools are given below. The reader is invited to examine how the innovative practice in these schools might apply to his or her own school setting and evolving RCs. The latter three schools were visited as a part of the London Gifted and Talented and NACE Project titled *Raising the Achievement of Able, Gifted and Talented Pupils within an Inclusive School Framework*.

Case study I: Belper School, Derbyshire

Belper School and Sixth Form Centre (www.belperschool.co.uk/cms/) is located in central Derbyshire providing a mixed, comprehensive education to about 1500 pupils. I have visited the school regularly since 1975 and have always been highly impressed by the positive, friendly attitudes and inclusiveness of students and staff. This is a school where pupils are not required to wear a set uniform and where pupils can address staff by their first names.

During 2002–2003 the SMT at Belper School agreed to host a pioneering year-long project in which six secondary-aged pupils (three older girls and three younger boys) formed a dedicated group with a teacher, meeting mostly on a fortnightly basis in a room with protected time. They all felt themselves to be underachieving at school. That group had most of the key attributes of a RC without carrying that particular name or identity per se. Their considerable narrative and accomplished productivity has been summarised in *Children at the Margins: Supporting Children, Supporting Schools* (Billington and Pomerantz, 2004: Chapter 11). While a great deal of advanced written preparation was drafted mainly to justify its operations for the SMT, this proved to be rather unnecessary. The student members were pretty certain that they did not need much in the way of training in how to conduct student-based school research. They simply wanted to get started with the project utilising skills and staff expertise already at their disposal. They wanted their work to be local and not to be labelled as NGIE ('no good . . . invented elsewhere'). The group was stable, self-disciplined and chose not to expand beyond the original cohort except for one late entry.

Within the initial meetings, they addressed self-selected topics such as boredom and apathy in the classroom and consequent underachievement, and they were inclined to believe that overall school attainments could be raised substantially if there was a better partnership between the teachers and those being taught. Again a 'cat and mouse' game where power is normally vested in the hands of staff was deemed to be unhelpful. This is a school that prides itself on exemplary staff/student relationships. The group seemed very familiar with teaching and learning styles, creativity, mind maps and the pressure on staff to meet exam targets. They spoke of a mismatch between preferred learning styles and what they as G + T pupils were being offered. They felt that their lessons employed mostly visual and auditory teaching styles while the kinaesthetic (K) or practical 'hands-on' approaches appeared to be reserved for pupils with special educational needs (SENs). They were seeking a richer 'K' diet as applied to the SENs pupils and did not feel the need to research this in a traditional academic manner.

Their plan was to hold a student teacher day in the Summer term of 2003, and they managed to sell the idea to the SMT and recruit about forty volunteer student teachers from Belper School who would take over a cross-section of lessons on that particular day. The event was publicised in advance so the rest of the pupils knew how the contact worked. If the classes were well-behaved, the lesson would be taught entirely by the student teacher with the usual adult teacher carefully observing from the back of the room. The presence of the regular teacher as the observer was crucial. If the student teacher somehow appeared to be losing control of the class, the regular teacher would take over. Fortunately, this was not necessary, and the comprehensive written evaluations of what happened on the day were overwhelmingly positive.

The key to the success of the day was the preliminary planning conversations which took place in advance. The student teacher enquired as to what lesson content and anticipated learning outcomes needed to be addressed for a given session, and then demonstrated how he or she, acting alone or with a partner, would like to teach the lesson with a more experiential or 'hands-on' approach. In essence, the student teachers wanted the regular adult teachers to see and to experience personally how the pupils would like to be taught with a richer 'K' style of curriculum delivery. In most cases these conversations were productive. Where lessons were assessed as being less successful by the younger recipients, it could be attributed to a lack of care in the planning before the teaching. Taking conversational short cuts did not work effectively and potentially defeated the purpose of the day, which was designed to foster better collaboration by givers and receivers of teaching.

The six core G + T members were pleased with the day's work and how the adults learned from the process. Their hope was that in future there would be greater planning communication between those teaching and those being taught, about teaching and learning styles and how to encourage greater K activity. They appreciated that not all staff would have been singularly impressed with the day, but they felt that a standard had been set and a model had been demonstrated. The work throughout the year was quietly facilitated by adults who supported the work but left much to the discretion of the members.

The following three site visit reports highlight examples of excellent G + T practice which includes ideas for developing RCs from one-to-one discourse between teachers and students, to wider evidence-based projects.

Case study 2: Lampton School, London Borough of Hounslow

Lampton School (www.lampton.hounslow.sch.uk/) is located in central Hounslow and provides a mixed, comprehensive education to a truly multi-cultural population of 1382 pupils ranging in age from 11 to 18. This figure includes 315 pupils in the Sixth Form. It is a now a very popular school and is oversubscribed.

Applicants feel privileged to gain a place here. As part of the Raising Achievement Project, on arrival, I met a Year 8 pupil at the edge of the vast campus and was escorted to Reception by someone endowed with great respect and appreciation for the whole educational community. Her unrehearsed, friendly, spontaneous and quite voluntary commentary provided a splendid introduction to all that would follow. She spoke with convincing authority and considerable enthusiasm for all that the school provides not only with the curriculum but also within the essential life of the school. What she foretold in the space of a few memorable minutes was matched by a succession of innovative, honest, balanced and constructive interviews and meetings with a cross- section of various stakeholders, each of whom supported the aims and the mission of Lampton School.

In talking with school representatives, it is apparent that this school particularly values social and cultural diversity and this is reflected throughout the campus amongst the pupils, the staff and everything that meets the eye or reaches the ear. There is also a very strong emphasis placed upon both social justice and social mobility. Pupils feel safe, valued, included and are listened to by adults in a manner that demonstrates a high level of real community participation, rather than empty and patronising clichés about simply listening to the 'voice of the child' which all schools would claim to be doing these days. The school has an Equalities Group to examine and monitor all equalities' issues, such as the effectiveness of anti-bullying protocols, and to advise the HT about what is needed. The HT is proud to claim that her work is informed by what she hears from pupils. This is an inspiring research laboratory for participatory learning about democracy and citizenship.

The G + T facilities and resources have grown over the past ten years at Lampton School. The current G + T coordinator has raised the gifted and talented profile so that it has become infused within the school culture and is no longer considered a 'bolt on' additional feature, but is more a part of mainstream school life, and G + T policies are seen to benefit all pupils rather than just a few.

Lampton School has a G + T register with about 10 per cent of the school population on it. It provides a very rich diet of extension and enrichment activities for all its pupils. It would claim that any particular opportunities that are specifically created for the G + T community are also open and available to other pupils, so that G + T pupils are not seen as privileged in some way that would compromise the school's policy about equal opportunities for all. The G + T coordinator takes a lead role in G + T innovations and maintenance, but this work is supported by many other staff who share equal enthusiasm about reducing underachievement across the curriculum. The school hosts many visitors every year and is open to the wider community and to ideas and suggestions that originate from beyond its walls and borders. It is an enlightened and exciting place for the whole locality and prides itself on working with many partners; providing a challenging training opportunity for new teachers to learn how to teach in the presence of talented, experienced role models. While senior managers are pleased with their exam results, they appreciate the need to look for constant improvements.

The G + T coordinator has a rolling programme of raising the G + T profile and emphasising personalised learning amongst staff and pupils. While the initial focus was upon stressing the importance of G + T identification, through the development and maintenance of departmental plans and self- assessment, and the G + T register, the emphasis has shifted to a much closer analysis of the teaching and learning processes. One example highlights recent commitments. Following work completed at the Cambridge Academy on Critical Thinking in March 2006, staff participated in an 'Engaging the Mind at KS5' Continuous Professional Development event at their Sandbanks Conference in September 2006. Teachers were encouraged to examine processes such as metacognition, challenge, problem-solving, construction of knowledge, conceptual learning, analysis and questioning to see how these could be encouraged within departments to achieve a deeper level of learning with pupils. This is exemplary evidence of a broad and thriving staff-based RC in action.

Attenders were encouraged to look at critical thinking and to see how this might be developed at Lampton School across the campus. One outcome was the creation of the Critical Thinking Study Group which produced a report on 17 January 2007 looking at the application of critical thinking across departments, with reflections and suggestions for further development. While this activity was primarily applicable to sixth formers, the consequences can, and will, have wide-ranging effects upon 'learning to learn' with regard to younger pupils as the thinking is easily generalised. It is particularly characteristic of Lampton that while the fuse was lit by the G + T coordinator, the project was developed, owned and instituted by enthusiastic teachers rather than simply imported from elsewhere. This development work is not finished, but it is already helping students to stretch themselves and achieve a deeper understanding of subject material and the learning process. This work will be self-sustaining. This experience with the methodology and the process is a stimulant for future critical reflection and improvements. The challenge is to design programmes to reach those pupils who appear to engage less with critical thinking. Some staff are looking at the amount of information they present to their students and the pace with which learning takes place.

The G + T policy is to adopt a whole-school approach that positively affects the entire community. There is no doubt that the emphasis placed upon developing thinking and 'learning to learn' skills is equally applicable to all Lampton School pupils. There is an acknowledgement of needing to meet the needs of twice exceptional (2E) pupils. These are pupils who would be exceptional in being G + T but would also be exceptional in another way such as having special educational needs (SENs) such as dyslexia, being a Looked After Child (LAC), being a 'hard to reach' young person, having mental health problems or being at risk of exclusion.

Provision for G + T pupils pervades the school and is embedded within the fabric of school life. It is not marginalised or sidelined. In the past, pupils have had access to G + T summer schools both on campus and elsewhere. G + T pupils, like all other pupils, benefit from raised expectations, personalised learning and performance targets which are set in consultation with pupils, teachers and parents and reviewed regardless of underachievement. This is an opportunity for celebration and not just for seeking improvement. When a pupil's progress is reviewed, all his or her teachers inform that process with up-to-date contributions. Discussions are held within departments, looking at patterns and areas for improvement, challenge and innovation. Responsibilities are made clear to all stakeholders. Conversations with pupils allow them to take an active role in examining strengths and weaknesses of learning programmes and homework. Pupils have an opportunity to influence this reflective process and to seek appropriate help from the staff. They help to set and evaluate challenges and to indicate what they value and where their education is heading. This is designed to heighten motivation and passion for learning. This also allows the school to exploit the intellectual capital of its G + T population and avoid lost opportunities.

During the visit, I heard many positive narratives about activities that had touched the lives of the pupils. A few of the many activities cited, include:

- winning mock elections;
- studying Latin (which is growing in popularity);
- designing and editing a newspaper;
- engaging in debates;
- accepting challenges and initiating projects;
- compiling a 'Stories of School Life' magazine about some work abroad in Kampala, Uganda;
- winning competitions;

- visiting universities;
- working within Virtual Learning Environments (VLEs);
- participating in science and philosophy clubs;
- pupils actually teaching lessons;
- accessing and supporting others through mentoring.

One young pupil proudly won a major debating event by constructing a Marxist interpretation about the Battle of Hastings. Talent like this in any setting needs to be nurtured, so the school can reap the benefits of pupil contributions to solving problems.

The school *2005* Ofsted Report (2005: 51), cites:

> Gifted and talented students are offered a successful film making course out of school hours. Last year four students won a media competition which enabled them to go to Pakistan and meet the President. At the last inspection, media studies was considered a strength of the school and it remains so.

The school atmosphere is buzzing with purposeful activity and goal-oriented behaviour within the student body. Morale is high and evident. In my formal interview, appointments with students and more casual class observations and other settings, such as the school cafeteria, I witnessed commitment, enthusiasm, pride and considerable participatory ownership and investment in the school as a social community. These pupils do not look like visitors who simply and passively join the school for a few years to endure an education controlled by staff. They really value the extra effort made by their teachers and they rise to the challenge. They appreciate that an education is not simply a matter of acquisition of a body of facts to be reproduced within examinations. They know that it is equally important to gain 'learning to learn' skills to prepare for all that life will throw at them later. They are well aware that their behaviour and their academic and vocational attainments are under close scrutiny and that they will not be allowed to 'slip though the net' educationally. They know that parents will also be closely involved in the process.

Within staff, parent and pupil conversations, there is widespread evidence of ongoing assessment for learning. The pupils certainly seem to understand and appreciate the process and the outcome and aspirations. There is consistent attribution of control being accepted by the students themselves. No one suggests that this is someone else's problem to sort out. Pupils can sense the logic and intent behind self-assessment as a process. When asked the perennial question about causes for classroom boredom at school, the pupils are inclined to take some responsibility onto their own shoulders for any lessons deemed less than inspiring. They can see that ownership of some of the problems might spell dividends in terms of repairing a lesson that is at risk because of the behaviour of one disruptive pupil. They can see a role for pupils in joining a RC designed to look into classroom behaviour.

Resources are deployed to allow G + T developments to occur in an orderly manner. Pupils play a role in informing G + T innovations, and the voices of the G + T pupils are eagerly solicited, carefully heard and appropriately acted upon. G + T systems are not confined to a marginalised location on the campus but percolate throughout the school and are continuing to develop. Substantial amounts of staff time are dedicated to the growing G + T agenda within planned continuous professional development time. Periodic audits such as the NQS Self Assessment allow staff to reflect upon strengths and weaknesses of G + T activity.

The staff at Lampton School appreciate that there is no simple and singular cause to account for underachievement even though there is commitment to minimise its effects. They accept that school is only a part in the lives of their 11 to 18-year-old students and that there are many other influences, such as the family, the peer group and the media, that can impact on motivation and attainment. Staff are ever vigilant to screen and identify any pupil who is at risk of working below his or her potential and then to initiate conversations with pupils, staff and family members to devise a differentiated or personalised intervention that addresses that specific risk. Girls receive as much attention as boys in this area.

Reflection is a shared undertaking and one that is done seriously and with some formality. There are a variety of steps that are taken to examine the curriculum, the strategies to deliver that curriculum, targets, learning styles, homework styles, deadlines, peer influence (positive and negative), compliance procedures, help seeking, packages of support and the specific raising or lowering of staff expectations where appropriate. This is built upon a systems perspective that acknowledges pupil vulnerability and weaknesses. It is positive and collaborative. It raises hopes and aspirations. It accepts factors that are both within and external to the pupil. It can be restorative and therapeutic. Pupils are encouraged to seek out individual teachers when underachievement is first identified so as to minimise the chance of this escalating. This is what one might expect of a community that achieves what it sets out to accomplish.

Case study 3: Newstead Wood School for Girls, Orpington, Kent

Newstead Wood School for Girls (www.newsteadwood.bromley.sch.uk/) is a Foundation, Selective, 11–18 Engineering Specialist School with a particular focus on the application of science, mathematics and technology. It is located in Orpington within the London Borough of Bromley. Admissions are based upon an application to the school and the local authority, a residence within a given radius of the school and both verbal and non-verbal reasoning tests, which take place annually in November. Successful applicants have scores within the top 130 places and about 750 pupils apply each year. Newstead Wood draws pupils from over sixty primary schools. There are over 950 pupils in this educational setting. The school has a rich and diverse student body that places great emphasis on racial equality and social justice. Thirty-five per cent of the pupils are from various ethnic minorities. It never excludes pupils, which is exceptional.

Newstead Wood have prioritised developing the G + T agenda across the whole-school operations and the entire curriculum. They are doing very well and they have robust plans to do even better. The evidence can be seen within their overall School Development Plans where they set an objective to promote their school as a centre of excellence for G + T. They have developed a range of partnerships and work with London Challenge. They engage in research and pilot projects and disseminate good practice internally and externally. There are three G + T coordinators in the school.

Furthermore, it classifies its 'exceptionally able' as pupils who meet general and subject criteria which are set by departments, as well as by looking at a range of quantitative data. These are publicised in their booklet entitled 'Identification of Gifted and Talented (Exceptionally Able) Students'.

There can be no doubt that departments are using multiple criteria and sources of evidence to identify exceptional pupils, and they maintain a paper trail showing how identification and subsequent teaching intervention are working, and are having an measurable impact across departments. Students are encouraged to be involved in these processes. G + T coordinators are vigilant to see that identification is robust and improving. The subject specific register of the 'exceptionally able' is incorporated in the Aim High programme database containing student assessment information.

Staff do not see the G + T work as an additional feature to be addressed when time permits, but more as an integral part of the whole teaching process. The strategy is personalised in terms of day-to-day teaching, and the production of regular progress reports and target setting with pupils three times each year.

This is where underachievement is addressed. Staff look very closely at any discrepancy between a pupil's targets and current performance. If a pupil is underperforming, there is a serious conversation that attempts to identify a good intervention strategy, such as, finding a mentor, examining the problems within the work, or altering expectations or work styles. There is also a very close review of schemes of work within departments.

The personalising of learning is particularly relevant if a pupil is not making progress against set targets; here pupils and teachers engage in a dialogue to elucidate what needs to be changed. The pupils I consulted feel that their teachers are fully engaged with them in both group and individual school activities, and that staff always have time to listen and to talk. The parents I consulted reflect the same personalised aspects to the learning. Written records and computer databases back up this communication. The SMT are vigilant with regards to a systems G + T approach and they take an interest in any area where there is vulnerability or risk of underachievement.

It is particularly impressive to witness how extensively inclusion underlies the philosophy and the ethos of the school environment. The girls have elected to apply to this popular and oversubscribed single-gender setting, and do not see themselves disadvantaged by the absence of boys in the classrooms. They take social justice issues seriously and appreciate how the voice of the pupil is represented politically within school. They have an interest in democratic processes and demonstrate considerable pride in the school's values and principles. They were consulted about possibly changing the school's Mission Statement, but stated that little improvement is needed. This reflects the fact that pupils were involved in the original drafting of the statement.

The staff see G + T identification as a means to an end and that the process of improving the education of the 'exceptionally able' has benefited the whole-school community. The honesty and critical reflection about teaching and learning that is constantly taking place with enthusiasm and commitment is convincingly impressive. The staff are as interested in the questions as the answers. They feel valued and supported in this challenging work.

Within individual lessons, pupils report and demonstrate a thirst for learning and demonstrate pride and ownership in what they do. They are good ambassadors for the school. They appear to agree to conform as is necessary, and they positively credit their teachers for the way the lessons are prepared and managed. They particularly value teachers who achieve the appropriate balance between being overly strict or overly lenient, and they show great respect for teachers who bring passion to their subject. They appreciate the privilege and the opportunity to be in an educational institution that consistently achieves very high national examination results, and they feel that the school is genuinely interested in the education and the welfare of *all* its pupils. This is what makes their school feel unique and distinct.

The school does use setting in Maths within year groups to facilitate differentiation. Lessons are structured to utilise a variety of teaching and learning methods which students appreciate. They value good introductions and demonstrations followed by opportunities to engage in practical approaches, problem-solving, group work, projects, research, homework, etc.

Staff personalise the academic and practical tasks by:

- the questions they set;
- the help they offer;
- the inspiration they provide;
- the expectations they have of students;
- the time they allow for work production;
- the degree to which they offer help;
- the homework assigned;
- the use of critical feedback and praise.

It is certainly not the case that all students in a given cohort are treated the same. Staff know they are held accountable for how much they can demonstrate this personalised learning in their classrooms. Much of the school decision-making is informed by contributions that originate within various focus groups. There is one that is specific to the G + T cohort.

The examination results show a portfolio of work that demonstrates the output of a large cross-section of pupils' activity over their final terms within secondary education. Newstead Wood has the highest entry figures for Oxbridge in the London area. This is not achieved by reputation alone, but by concerted efforts on the part of the staff and the pupils over a period of years. It is not the result of some final cramming to do well in exams, but it is more a statement of the emphasis that is placed upon complex knowledge construction. These students are given enormous opportunities over many years and they appear to take full advantage of these.

It would be fair to stipulate that almost all the Newstead Wood pupils would be classified as G + T if they were enrolled in a typical comprehensive school. As a school population, they do exceptionally well at GCSE, at A level and in a variety of outside school activities that are fully celebrated. The 'exceptionally able' pupils are likewise benefiting substantially from the opportunities provided and are working to their potential and the high expectations that their teachers set for them.

The staff have well-constructed development plans that are both general and specific to the G + T population. They conduct audits to see where improvements can be made. Whenever asked how they can support their opinions with hard evidence, they produce written documentation compiled to a high standard. The new development plans are informed by evaluating previous plans, assessing performance indicators and listening to individual and group pupil feedback. Newstead Wood is a listening organisation. It works through a cycle of self-assessments and makes changes as and where appropriate. Teamwork is very much in evidence and there is a high level of morale within the staff and the student body.

Staff and pupils engage in a constructive educational dialogue about how they communicate with reference to:

*   academic tasks;
*   motivation;
*   anxieties;
*   projects;
*   challenges;
*   work–life balance;
*   personal research;
*   personal work portfolios;
*   extracurricular activities;
*   work styles;
*   homework management;
*   course options choices;
*   careers guidance.

There is no doubt that the students are active participants within this important dialogue. Pupils know they need to prepare and to account for what they are doing. Pupils are inclined to attribute success and failure to their own decision-making rather than blaming other factors such as the teachers or the curriculum. They seem to value how to negotiate with staff and how to use their own initiative. What they think and believe in terms of their own self-assessments, critical reflections and target settings seems to predominate. These regular conversations appear to take place on both a formal and an informal basis. What the school staff provide in the way of qualitative and quantitative data to inform these discussions is appreciated. There is potential for pupils to take responsibility to repair conversations with teachers when somehow the discussions are not achieving the potential that is possible.

There is a developing research culture within the school and staff are personally encouraged to gather data that can be used to improve delivery of the curriculum. One example is titled 'The impact of extension topics aimed at exceptionally able students on the achievements of these students and on all the students within that class'. This comprehensive twenty-two-page study shows evidence of seeking the views of pupils, careful interpretation of the data, critical reflection and evidence that an experiment with extension tasks led to embedding work within the normal course work for the coming year. This is but one example of how staff are encouraged to improve their practice via supported research in school.

Unlike some G + T coordinators in other schools who appear to have to sell the G + T agenda or have to battle for resources and managerial time and consideration, the social context at Newstead Wood places the needs of the G + T community right at the heart of the school and its forward developmental planning. These staff are involved in the construction of school G + T policy, the day-to-day practice and the G + T provision. Staff are fully involved and consulted at all levels in this school. Policy is reviewed with stakeholders regularly. There is a G + T focus group to inform the process. The pupils at Newstead Wood School speak with conviction about how their voices are heard and how they can employ their talents to contribute to school life. This dynamic and developmental G + T policy contains a rationale, strategic objectives and operational objectives.

Some concern was expressed about underachievement as all staff are keen to identify and remedy, where possible, cases of underachievement. From a systems perspective the staff are currently doing just about everything possible to minimise underachievement amongst their pupils. They have in place very intricate procedures to identify underachieving G + T pupils, to monitor their progress and to intervene when necessary and advisable in the light of suspected underachievement.

Staff are aware that within a school that sets and achieves such high academic standards, there are risks that some pupils will be particularly vulnerable to psychological problems involving stress, anxiety, low self-esteem and excessive self-criticism. They take steps to address these issues, and students and parents feel this is generally quite effective.

When underachievement is found, the meeting between the pupil and the teacher is the appropriate place to explore one of a variety of interventions that might result in a new approach to learning. Parents can become involved when necessary but the emphasis is upon nurturing the independence of the pupil and the promotion of an adult model of education. Students are expected to maintain a portfolio of achievement which incorporates reports.

A few pupils would be targeted as candidates for additional staff attention and intervention where this is deemed valuable. Sometimes, it has to be acknowledged that the cause of some underachievement can lie within personal circumstances outside the control of the school. In these cases counselling is available both within the school and externally.

When a trend is noted within a group, then staff collaborate and look to group solutions, such as, reorganising schedules of work, raising expectations, lowering anxieties, revisiting departmental policies and resources, providing staff training and staff support and instigating research to further elucidate the cause of the underachievement. Generally, the staff take proactive measures to prevent or minimise underachievement before it happens. The SMT are constantly assessing the impact of all school policies with regard to vulnerable pupils, and they take preventative action where it is felt to be warranted. This is reflected in the annual construction of the school development plan.

Case study 4: Seven Kings School, Ilford, Essex

The school motto is Friendship, Excellence and Opportunity. Seven Kings High School (http://public.skhs.net/) in the London Borough of Redbridge in Ilford is a Sixth Form entry, 11–18, coeducational, mixed ability, multi-ethnic, comprehensive school with about 1440 pupils on roll of whom about 470 are in the sixth form.

Staff are particularly proud of their involvement on the 'Learn how to Learn' project with a key focus on 'Assessment for Learning' – a national action research project on assessment and learning. They also play a big role in training teachers both on and off the school site. There are about 70–80 languages spoken within the overall community. The school has a rich and diverse student body that places great emphasis on inclusion, equal opportunities, racial equality and social justice. Parents and members of the local community feel welcomed, listened to and valued.

Seven Kings High School place a great emphasis on developing the G + T agenda with enthusiasm, and this would apply throughout the school. The G + T coordinator is an assistant HT with SMT responsibilities and influence, who has numerous contacts outside the school and who sees research and pilot projects as vital to school developments.

Staff are given extensive training, advice and guidance on how to structure lessons to challenge G + T pupils and how to rephrase questions seeking higher order thinking skill development.

Staff are also given guidance about how best to look out for G + T pupils in individual lessons. A cohort of between 5 and 10 per cent of every year group is identified by staff as G + T. Teachers are held responsible for identification, appropriate teaching and the monitoring of progress. Schemes of work have a range of activities to bolster tasks already being done as well as stand-alone tasks that would benefit G + T pupils. The SMT expects all staff to see this as an entitlement. They look for differential rates of progression for those pupils who can learn faster with deeper understanding.

Departments are expected to work closely with the school's G + T coordinator to self-assess against National Quality Standards (NQS) and they do this through an audit. Staff have a clear view of procedures, the ownership of responsibilities and what is expected of them. They do not see the G + T work as an additional feature to be addressed when time permits, but more as an integral part of the whole teaching process. The strategy is personalised in terms of day-to-day teaching, the production of regular progress reports and target setting with pupils three times each year. This is where the identification of underachievement is addressed. Staff look very closely at any discrepancy between a pupil's targets and current performance. If a pupil is underperforming, there would be a planned conversation that attempts to identify a good intervention such as finding a mentor, examining the problems within the work or altering expectations or work styles. There is also a very close review of schemes of work within departments.

The personalising of student work is particularly relevant if a pupil is not making progress against set targets. Here they engage in a dialogue to elucidate what needs to be changed. The pupils feel that their teachers are fully engaged with them in both group and individual school activities and that staff always have time to listen and to talk. Written records and computer databases back up this communication. The SMT are vigilant with regards to a systems G + T approach and they take an interest in any area where there is perceived vulnerability or risk of underachievement.

Inclusion extensively underlies the philosophy and the ethos of the school. The pupils and their parents reflect a strong sense of pride in belonging to a progressive and nationally recognised educational facility. They feel that the school's efforts to identify G +T pupils and their needs are outstanding. The voice of the child is recognised and is enshrined in the school's culture and its operations. They have an interest in democratic processes and demonstrate considerable pride in the school's values and principles. The honesty and critical reflection about teaching and learning in evidence reflects enthusiasm and commitment. They feel valued and supported in this challenging work.

Once the G + T pupils are identified and their work is monitored, the staff reflect on how challenged pupils are both in the classroom and outside the classroom. All G + T pupils are given targets and in the regular meetings with their teachers, they can look at the congruence between what has been expected academically in terms of targets and what has been accomplished in a manner that relies on hard evidence and teachers' opinions. Sometimes targets need to be reviewed and possibly modified.

G + T pupils are expected to move beyond the basics of answering questions such as 'who, what, when, where, why and how' and they are encouraged to examine challenges with higher order thinking skills involving analysis, synthesis, application and the generation of knowledge rather than simply returning what has been given. The pupils appear to value and actually experience practical, experiential or 'hands-on' interactive learning. They are given opportunities to learn about how to learn. The acquisition of research and communication competencies is highly valued. It feels very much like an adult model of education, especially as these G + T pupils progress to the advanced years in school. They participate in forum meetings about learning where their voices are communicated to the SMT. The students' voices are valued, and a G + T forum is about to be established. Students are encouraged to write stories for the news bulletin and some reports celebrate accomplishments achieved in competitions away from school. Debate is popular and this is one area where G + T pupils can be really stretched.

There is thriving 'out of hours' enrichment programme convened during the lunch hour and after school, including a very wide variety of performance-related activities in music, drama and dance, sports (football, netball, basketball, cricket, athletics, swimming, cross country and rounders) and clubs such as music, chess, sailing, biology, etc. The school won the 'Sportsmark' for its high level of pupil participation in sport. Pupils have the opportunity to engage in many school trips to museums, galleries, foreign countries, skiing, residential courses and outdoor pursuit activities. Engaging in video-conferences with links to universities is a poplar activity. A lot was heard about the Salter's Festival of Chemistry and the enthusiasm noted for forensic investigations. One pupil reported experiencing 'decompression' following a NAGTY event where the tuition was so enlightening she found readjusting to her normal classes very difficult.

There is an incredibly wide range of enriching and innovative educational opportunities available for every G + T pupil. It must be quite a challenge to make a decision as to what to join and what to save for another year. Master classes are popular. They have run successful summer schools for G + T pupils from Years 6 to 8.

The examination results show a portfolio of work that demonstrates the output of a large cross-section of pupils' activity over their final terms within secondary education. This is not achieved by reputation alone, but by concerted efforts on the part of the staff and the pupils over a period of years. These students are given enormous opportunities over many years and they appear to take full advantage of this.

Every year, staff evaluate their G + T teaching and provision. The school's G + T coordinator liaises with all departments and expects them to audit standards and to look for areas of vulnerability where G + T pupils could be taught differently to achieve even higher standards. He expects each department to develop plans and to keep him informed as to their needs and progress. Each department sets its own G + T targets and these are reviewed regularly within a self-assessment procedure. Staff are aware that some G + T pupils could benefit from greater challenge and they are working on this. They see this as an important school development task.

Pupil progress is monitored each term by reports which compare achievements and effort. The Seven Kings staff have a great interest in Assessment for Learning (AfL). They see assessing work and carefully orchestrated feedback to pupils as a key opportunity to challenge G + T pupils and to ask more high-level questions that probe for a better understanding of what a given pupil has learned and where the pupil might need specific tuition. An example might be 'This is what you did and this is what you need to do.' They see close links between AfL and the promotion of the National Quality Standards in G + T education. Peer assessments are also promoted and highly valued.

In terms of forward planning, staff are asked to improve the pupil tracking, to get pupils to design their own tasks and to look into ways in which this is done effectively. Some examples were demonstrated of how all staff can access a vast array of quantitative and qualitative pupil-specific data to inform their target setting, tracking and reporting of progress. This includes comments about concerns.

Staff engage in constructive educational dialogue and they communicate frequently about academic tasks, motivation, anxieties, projects, challenges, personal research, personal work portfolios, extracurricular activities, work styles, homework management, course options choices, careers guidance, etc. There is no doubt that the students are active participants within these conversations. Pupils know they need to prepare and to account for what they are doing. They value negotiating with staff and using their own initiative. What they think and believe in terms of their own self-assessments, critical reflections and target settings predominate.

These conversations take place on both a formal and an informal basis. What the school staff provide in the way of qualitative and quantitative data to inform these conversations is valued and appreciated. Staff carry specific responsibilities for data acquisition, maintenance, security and information dissemination as and where appropriate. The extensive school IT facilities support this work.

The intention is that assessment shows progression within each subject and that this information is shared with pupils and parents. Pupil self-assessment complements other types of assessment and encourages students to carry personal responsibility for their progress. The staff use both Assessment for Learning (formative assessment) and Assessment of Learning (summative assessment.)

There is a research culture within the school, and staff are personally encouraged to gather data that can be used to improve curricular planning and delivery of the curriculum.

The G + T coordinator is credited with giving the G + T a very strong emphasis across the whole-school community. He leads by example and sets high expectations amongst the teachers. He wants to be kept well informed about both successes and any suggestions to improve teaching for G + T pupils. Departments are expected to self-assess against the NQS, to review their plans, to set new targets each year and to report back to the G + T coordinator. He always wants to know what steps each department intend to take with the G + T agenda in the months ahead. The G + T pupil forum and increased coaching and mentoring of the G + T are planned. All staff have specific G + T training, focusing on both identification and how to further challenge G + T. Staff training is planned, focusing more on acquiring skills rather than knowledge. This is systemically built into induction for NQTs. There are plans to offer Open University modules to pupils in the sciences.

Staff are fully involved and consulted at all levels about G + T policies and practices in this school. G + T policy is generated, monitored and maintained by the SMT, and the school governors are very supportive of it. Staff, parents and pupils are proud of what is accomplished at Seven Kings High School. The school has a low exclusion rate and prides itself on its inclusive policies and practices.

A summary of key factors with regard to successful school provision is below:

- An active school credo of Friendship, Excellence, Opportunity.
- A focus on developing skills for Learning how to Learn.
- An emphasis on Assessment for Learning resulting in Differentiated Provision.
- A policy of inclusion.
- An emphasis on Equal Opportunities, Racial Equality, Social Justice.
- Regular targeting Professional Development.
- Active Student Voice with Ownership of Learning.
- Extensive Out-of-hours Learning.
- Widespread Community Involvement.

Conclusion

Readers are encouraged to look for signs of emerging RCs in various forms in local schools and to offer encouragement and tactful support where it is needed. It does not require much adult input to set the wheels in motion and then observe what can be achieved when a few G + T pupils are given a greater voice in how to improve education for themselves and their peers. RCs can thrive without much positive influence or negative interference coming from outside the school or from adult staff. Every RC needs to develop its own identity and place its own signature on its work. They need to establish their own priorities. Their actions should not threaten any staff but should afford them the opportunity to observe how creativity and spontaneity can flourish in a host community that values initiative and critical, reflective thought processes. There is nothing stopping staff from forming their own RCs.

Able underachievers continue to complain that too much about school is boring and that their time is being wasted. RCs offer some considerable scope to redress problems and to give ownership of some school problems to those with the strongest vested interests to recommend school improvements.

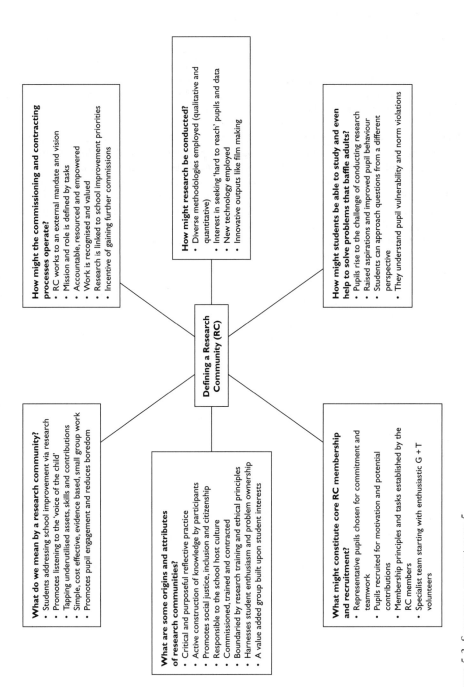

What do we mean by a research community?
- Students addressing school improvement via research
- Promotes listening to the 'voice of the child'
- Tapping underutilised assets, skills and contributions
- Simple, cost effective, evidence based, small group work
- Promotes pupil engagement and reduces boredom

What are some origins and attributes of research communities?
- Critical and purposeful reflective practice
- Active construction of knowledge by participants
- Promotes social justice, inclusion and citizenship
- Responsible to the school host culture
- Commissioned, trained and contracted
- Boundaried by research training and ethical principles
- Harnesses student enthusiasm and problem ownership
- A value added group built upon student interests

How might the commissioning and contracting processes operate?
- RC works to an external mandate and vision
- Mission and role is defined by tasks
- Accountable, resourced and empowered
- Work is recognised and valued
- Research is linked to school improvement priorities
- Incentive of gaining further commissions

Defining a Research Community (RC)

How might research be conducted?
- Diverse methodologies employed (qualitative and quantitative)
- Interest in seeking 'hard to reach' pupils and data
- New technology employed
- Innovative outputs like film making

What might constitute core RC membership and recruitment?
- Representative pupils chosen for commitment and teamwork
- Pupils recruited for motivation and potential contributions
- Membership principles and tasks established by the RC members
- Specialist team starting with enthusiastic G + T volunteers

How might students be able to study and even help to solve problems that baffle adults?
- Pupils rise to the challenge of conducting research
- Raised aspirations and improved pupil behaviour
- Students can approach questions from a different perspective
- They understand pupil vulnerability and norm violations

Figure 5.3 Summary concept map 5

References and further reading

Billington, T. and Pomerantz, M. (eds) (2004) *Children at the Margins: Supporting Children, Supporting Schools*. London: Trentham Books.

Department for Education and Skills (2007) *Gifted and Talented Education: Guidance on Preventing Underachievement: A Focus on Dual or Multiple Exceptionality (DME)*. Commissioned report. Ref: 00061-2007BKT-EN.

Freire, P. (1996) *Pedagogy of the Oppressed*. London: Penguin.

Neill, A. S. (1970) *Summerhill – A Radical Approach to Education*. Hove: Pelican.

Pomerantz, M. (2007) *Research Communities Debate*. (BPS/DECP) No. 122.

Pomerantz, M. (2007) 'A seminar approach to multi-agency collaboration, team building and therapeutic group problem solving where some attenders might be described as "Hard to Reach"', in Pomerantz, K., Hughes, M. and Thompson, D., *How to Reach 'Hard to Reach' Children*. Chichester: John Wiley and Sons.

Pomerantz, M. (2004) 'Belper School Able Underachievers Group 2002-2003', in Billington, T. and Pomerantz, M. (eds) *Children at the Margins: Supporting Children, Supporting Schools*. Stoke-on-Trent: Trentham Books Ltd.

Pomerantz, M. and Pomerantz, K. (2002) *Listening to Able Underachievers*. London: David Fulton.

Rogers, C. (2004) *On Becoming a Person*. London: Constable and Robinson, Ltd.

Wallace, B., Fitton, S. Leyden, S., Montgomery, D., Pomerantz, M. and Winstanley, C. (2007) *Raising the Achievement of Able, gifted and Talented Pupils within an Inclusive School Framework: Guidelines for Schools to Audit and Extend Existing Best Practice*. Oxford: National Association for Able Children in Education. publications@nace.co.uk

Chapter 6

Organisational strategies

Leadership and curriculum provision

Sally Fitton

Introduction

This chapter investigates the key features that underpin successful leadership and curriculum provision that constitute the significant drivers in tackling the underachievement of all pupils, including the more able. A range of common principles were found within the case-study schools and these are expanded in more detail here. The vision of the case-study schools is not one that clings to a narrow elitist view of recognising a small percentage of pupils as gifted and talented, but is one that is concerned to raise the achievement of all pupils within an inclusive context. The practitioners in these schools continually strive to provide more effective learning pathways for all, and in doing so, outstanding provision for gifted learners is being developed.

In the case-study schools, leaders create a safe environment within an ethos and climate of high aspirations, expectations and respect. This climate enables pupils to work in a variety of ways, collaboratively and individually, and to make decisions about their learning, allowing individual differences and achievements to be celebrated and valued.

Which qualities exemplify good leadership?

This section considers the impact of leadership in meeting the needs of all pupils including the gifted and talented.

Schools which have effective provision for gifted and talented pupils characteristically have a head and senior management team that strive for excellence, through setting high aspirations and expectations for all pupils. They ensure that staff understand that they have a collective responsibility for meeting the needs of the most able and encourage a whole-school approach addressing this agenda.

Leadership in the case-study schools is characterised by the elements of best practice outlined in Box 6.1.

Schools are cognisant of the broad guidelines of the National Quality Standards and also the detailed guidelines of best practice developed within the NACE Challenge Award. The NACE Challenge Award provides a

---

Box 6.1   Characteristics of good leadership

- The Every Child Matters, Personalised Learning and Inclusion Agendas are at the heart of everyday practice.
- Senior leaders create the right vision and ethos, culture and environment, whereby all children flourish.
- A culture of achievement is developed where the leadership has a strong and declared commitment to high standards.
- Pupils appreciate the ethos of high expectations which celebrates and rewards the multiple achievements of all pupils.
- The school policy ensures that coverage of gifted and talented provision is firmly embedded in practice.
- Robust monitoring and evaluation of the school's performance is regularly carried out.
- A planned programme of professional development is in place to support teachers in acquiring skills and expertise in developing appropriate provision.
- A Leading Teacher for gifted and talented plays an active supporting role.
- Class teachers who are leading learning and raising pupils' aspirations ensure that the curriculum provides challenge and motivates and engages all learners.
- Partnership in learning with pupils is a priority. Pupils are given the opportunity and responsibility for shaping their own learning. Parent partnerships are encouraged and they engage in regular reviews regarding their child's progress.
- Systematic identification and monitoring procedures of all pupils are in place and when underachievement is identified, appropriate intervention strategies are put in place.
- A vibrant curriculum is clearly evident in practice. Enrichment, extension and out-of-hours activities are rich and varied, catering for all pupils' needs.
- A dedicated governor is appointed who supports and challenges leadership in developing provision for able pupils.

---

framework which develops a whole-school approach to the process of developing provision using a wide range of tools and resources. Several of the case-study schools are working to achieve the NACE Challenge Award and are able to provide evidence of their systematic growth towards achieving the NACE accreditation.

Pedagogy and practice

> Personalising learning means in practical terms, focussing in a more structured way on each child's learning in order to enhance progress, achievement and participation. All children have the right to receive support and challenge, tailored to their needs, interests and abilities.
>
> (Christine Gilbert (2006) 2020 Vision)

What comes first?

The principles of good teaching for all pupils provides the basis for effective provision for gifted and talented learners. All pupils benefit from lessons that have pace, where teaching is personalised, inspirational and intellectually challenging. A key element in making effective provision for gifted and talented pupils is identifying each pupil's strengths and weaknesses and setting appropriate expectations, building in opportunities for them to perform beyond their age-related level.

It's pertinent at this point to reflect on the following question: Can we be really effective in identifying gifted and talented pupils if provision does not provide the opportunities for pupils to show/find their gifts and talents?

Evidence from the case-study schools suggests that they view identification as a continuous process which is interwoven with provision:

> Increasingly, identification should be viewed as part of good teaching, a continuous process that anticipates further challenging learning experiences with a quality end product. Seen in that way, identification is an evaluation process that teachers undertake in the classroom rather than [the administration of] a series of tests.
>
> (George, 2003)

The identification of pupil potential in the case-study schools relies on a variety of approaches that fall into six main categories which are prioritised in the following list:

- a curriculum that provides a wide variety of opportunities for individual pupils to discover their gifts and talents;
- teachers' professional assessments;
- consultation with parents;
- checklists of characteristic features;
- rigorous monitoring and tracking procedures;
- standardised tests of ability and attainment.

The case-study schools maintain that the most important aspect of provision for their able pupils is the day-to-day experience of teaching and learning in the classroom. Box 6.2 summarises the key elements in their daily provision for pupils.

REFLECT

Box 6.2   Key elements in successful daily provision for pupils

- Recognising individual learners' needs as a basis for curriculum planning.
- Ensuring clarity about progression in key concepts.
- Setting appropriate learning objectives and success criteria.
- Recognising that learning can take place in a variety of contexts and in a variety of ways.
- Monitoring and assessing pupils' progress to inform planning and teaching. Using Assessment for Learning frameworks.
- Involving pupils in target setting and monitoring their own progress.
- Working on the principle that personalised learning holds the key to the mainstreaming of gifted and talented education and provides the opportunity to develop provision which counteracts disadvantage and prevents underachievement.

Creating challenge in the classroom requires teachers to think flexibly, to find bespoke solutions to classroom problems and challenges, to take account of both general values and the aims of the school. Challenging provision is presented by the case-study schools through the recognition that pupils have a range of abilities, talents and learning styles that require a variety of opportunities and challenges for individuals to make the required progress. Teachers make practical judgements about the particular needs of individual learners, the different ways of organising people, the available technologies and, importantly, the culture in the classroom.

Debate on what constitutes challenging lessons has led to teachers identifying a list of 'ingredients' for creating effective and challenging lessons for the able, whilst supporting and extending all learners. Consider the elements in Box 6.3 and discuss how you might use it to extend your best practice.

REFLECT

Box 6.3   Key elements that teachers have found in effective and challenging lessons

- The children and young people understand and can discuss clearly observable or measurable progress in some aspect of their skills, knowledge and understanding. Coasting or underachievement is not acceptable.

- The teacher asks thoughtful, penetrating and enriching questions.
- Activities have depth of task as an essential feature.
- Careful and accurate Assessment for Learning enables the pupils to start from an appropriate base thus avoiding unnecessary repetition.
- Lessons have pace which enables challenging targets to be met.
- Time is used skilfully to promote depth of thought, allowing the pupils to revisit ideas and tasks in progress, enriching or extending them.
- Unexpected contributions from learners are valued.
- Lessons have a clear sense of purpose with time, space and resources well organised.
- Pupils are given the opportunity to make their own links and associations of ideas, drawing on their own skills, knowledge and understanding.
- Originality, creativity and imaginative thinking and problem-solving are recognised and reinforced.
- Self-esteem is of prime importance with pupils recognising 'mistakes' as key points in their learning.
- Pupils reflect on what has been learned and match it to the success criteria set at the beginning of the lesson.
- Learners are enabled to make meanings from their own experiences and findings. They make links between their existing or developing skills, knowledge and understanding, discovering new patterns of thinking or opportunities for further exploration.
- The opportunity is available for learners to continue the lesson or topic theme further if necessary.

Appropriate challenge provides tasks, assignments and questions that elicit higher-order responses: challenge is achieved by setting qualitatively different tasks rather than 'more-of-the-same'. What all the schools have in common is a shared understanding of the word 'learning' which relates to Saljo's six levels of learning:

1 Increase in knowledge
2 Memorising
3 Acquisition of facts to be retained and used when necessary
4 The abstraction of meaning
5 The interpretative process arrived at understanding reality
6 Changing as a person.

(Quoted in Bowden, 2003)

The first three levels result in 'shallow learning' and make little demand on able pupils. These three levels of teaching and learning focus the assessment on remembered information and on a predefined end product. Success in these areas often means that an able child has learnt very little that is new – getting ten out of ten in a spelling test does not show that 'deep' learning has taken place.

The last three levels of learning require higher levels of pupil involvement, as pupils draw together information and begin to perceive and make judgements and hypotheses. It is within these 'deep' areas of learning that able pupils are provided with the appropriate challenge.

Quality learning in the case-study schools is seen as a multifaceted process:

> Not simply increasing the store of knowledge, taking in and retaining more and more information. It's about searching for meaning, developing understanding and relating that understanding to the world around us.
>
> (Bowden, 2003)

At Ollerton Primary School, the development of the TASC Problem-Solving Framework (Thinking Actively in a Social Context) provides learners with both the framework and the opportunity to engage in a highly interactive teaching and learning process which changes according to individual needs; the learning tasks are adaptable and flexible. The main focus of TASC is on developing problem-solving and thinking skills; however, TASC also embraces quality initial teaching and experiential learning, building from a skilful design of individualised and group learning activities through flexible planning around a topic. There are times for direct instruction as well as times for open exploration and experiment. Different learning experiences are negotiated with the pupils and various strategies are used, such as visits and dialogue with experts, opportunities for individual research, negotiated and differentiated group work, a special time for reflection about learning, opportunities to rethink and change intentions and plans. This close interaction between teacher and learner can only happen within a safe, trusting environment.

Ollerton Primary School triggers learning that is sustained by curiosity, with a deliberate fostering of creativity, thinking, reasoning and problem-solving skills underpinned by increased knowledge and understanding.

The application of the TASC Framework develops not only cognitive skills but also social and interpersonal skills, by creating an environment for learning where pupils are taking more responsibility for their own decisions and actions. TASC supports positive behaviour for learning. Two boys explained how they worked together in a team and the importance of the role each had in the team, 'We get left behind as a team if we mess about, so we stay on task!' The TASC learning situation emphasises the value of learner talk and learner-initiated activity, making these the main avenues for learning;

there is an essential minimum of whole-class teacher-directed talk and clear rules for discussion and small group child-centred talk.

In both Portswood Primary School and Hermitage Primary school the teachers are developing provision which incorporates Renzulli's School-Wide Enrichment Model (The Schoolwide Enrichment Model (SEM), Renzulli, 1977).

In these two schools, lessons have a starting point which stimulates curiosity about a particular topic, problem or area of study. In this model, pupils are encouraged to adopt a problem-solving approach and to gather information, resources and strategies with which to explore and act on the problem. All pupils learn from the initial exploratory experience, while more able pupils develop higher-level thinking processes and are encouraged to develop research methodology, presentation of materials and critical evaluation. Pupils of varying abilities are challenged and supported in extending and excelling at the task they have undertaken. They agree individual targets and are given directions for improvement during lessons. Where under-achievement is identified then intervention plans are put in place. Box 6.4 contains a summary of the key factors that develop a school culture for challenge.

Box 6.4 Key factors that develop a school culture for challenge

- Secure general routine and a clear sense of purpose underlying activities.
- Warm, open and responsive relationships.
- An ethos which builds self-esteem and self-confidence.
- Assessment which ensures that the core skills of reading, writing, number work and information technology are secure and are being continually extended.
- Open expectations, with limits fixed by the potential of the learning activity and the capabilities of the child rather than by the teacher.
- Clear awareness of time-frames, the skilful use of pace and deadlines.
- Conscious fostering of the extension of projects, ideas and lines of enquiry.
- Valuing of enthusiasm and energy (even when misdirected!).
- Making changes of mind legitimate.
- Recognition that the unexpected is an essential part of open-ended enquiry.
- The predominant use of open-ended, real-life questions.

- Bringing high standards to the attention of the learners' pupils' own work and examples of high achievement from a wider range of real world contexts, for example, the work of acclaimed artists, engineers, writers and sports people.
- Promoting self-evaluation against rigorous and challenging criteria negotiated with the pupils.
- Respect for rational argument based on evidence, data and personal conviction.
- Establishing creditable failure as an integral part of the teaching and learning process.
- Seeing all solutions as provisional.
- Recognising and rewarding creativity and ingenuity; acknowledging the importance of imaginative and unusual approaches.
- Giving process a higher weighting than product and recognising this in the rewards system (planning, drafting, changing, altering, refining and improving).
- Ensuring depth of task in the activities provided.
- Taking opportunities to move the learners' thinking beyond the obvious; developing their ideas and findings with deeper questioning.
- Drawing the learners' thinking together around negotiated success criteria.
- Using the spiritual dimension of learners' thinking to enable them to make meaning from their ideas and findings.

In summary, all teachers in the case-study schools are providing tasks that are rich in possibilities: pupils are able to build on the initial engagement with a topic and to decide on extended areas of investigation. The pupils know their achievements are valued and they are allowed to work as individuals and in teams in the pursuit of their enquiries. The provision in the case-study schools presents challenges with breadth and depth. Pupils are provided with a rich range of resources and also encouraged to find their own. Learners are taught to hypothesise, to question, to explore open-ended investigations and to search for ideas and meanings beyond the concrete information.

Conclusion

All the factors identified in this chapter for ensuring appropriate provision for all pupils, including those with special needs, are linked and overlapping.

Dynamic, hands-on, committed leadership from senior management and subject leaders is essential in supporting teachers as they develop an educational system that is based on individual progression and is underpinned by assessment for learning principles. Essentially, pupil voice is a very important element in this negotiated development: all pupils know when their learning is interesting, motivating and engaging.

The case-study schools demonstrate the power of distributed leadership and shared responsibility and perceive the vital necessity of involving governors and parents/carers. In all the case-study schools, there is the feeling that everyone is involved, informed and responsible for the whole-school development. In other words there is a strong feeling of ownership and commitment fostered by regular acknowledgment of effort and by professional reflection with the will to rethink and improve organisation and provision.

The curricula in the case-study schools are based on the vision that all pupils have gifts and talents that need to be discovered and developed; although these gifts vary both in kind and in potential. The emphasis is on provision of curricula that are rich in opportunities and that focus on optimum progression for individual pupils. All the case-study schools focus on providing opportunities for out-of-hours learning, believing that school learning needs to be linked to lifelong learning.

All the schools in the research study make it clear that they have high expectations of staff and pupil progress: they plan for progression, differentiation and challenge. Teaching and learning are characterised by ambitious objectives, challenging targets, early intervention strategies which keep pupils on target, through the use of rigorous assessment procedures.

The following issues are intended for staff reflection in the light of existing best practice.

- Which facets of existing school leadership and organisation enable the successful implementation of the school action plan?
- What are the core values and implications of a truly inclusive curriculum? What challenges face teachers as they create a learning environment that meets the needs of the most able without excluding those pupils who need extra support?
- Do you agree that when specific attention is given to the needs of more able pupils there is often a general increase in the level of expectation for all pupils?
- Flexible lesson planning is the key to personalised provision. What evidence is there in existing planning to show that there are opportunities for personalised and differentiated learning?

REFLECT

Case studies

Case studies 1 and 2 illustrate the practice in two of the case-study primary schools. They are intended to provide practical examples for discussion and reflection. Case study 3 provides an example of flexible planning across the curriculum.

Case study 1: Ollerton Primary School

Contextual information

Ollerton Primary School (www.ollertonprimary.notts.sch.uk) has 300 pupils from Foundation to Year 6. The school has been in existence for two years after local reorganisation and serves one of the most disadvantaged wards within Nottinghamshire. There is high unemployment and high levels of social deprivation: nearly half the pupils are known to be eligible for free school meals and the number of pupils who are on the special needs register is well above the national average. There is high pupil mobility and a significant number of looked-after children with complex needs. With the majority of pupils being 'white' British there is an insignificant ethnic and cultural mix; there are no pupils with English as a second language.

The attainment of pupils on entry to full-time schooling is well below the local authority average for both literacy and numeracy. However, all pupils make good progress and the standards achieved by pupils are high in relation to similar schools and are improving steadily when compared to all schools.

The headteacher, teachers and governors set high expectations for all pupils and place a strong emphasis on inclusive approaches, providing variety and challenge for all pupils and identifying underachievement within all groups of pupils. Two years ago Ollerton School adopted a whole school approach across all phases using the Belle Wallace TASC Problem-solving and Thinking Skills Framework, which has enabled the school to develop and enrich the whole curriculum, both in school and in out-of-hours activities. The school data show that through effective leadership, providing a clear vision for learning, with an attractive stimulating environment, good teaching and strong relationships between all stakeholders, it is possible to ensure that pupils of all abilities can be equally successful in their learning.

Identification procedures

All staff have received training on the identification of able pupils using clear rationale which ensures consistency of approach. Once a pupil is identified then they are placed on a tentative and flexible G + T register, with teachers looking for any new talent to emerge in different contexts. Each pupil has a personal progress plan which is regularly monitored and amended. To assess attainment and progress, the school uses standardised group tests, together with observation reports from teachers; and subject coordinators have a role in monitoring able pupils across their subject. Meeting the needs of more able pupils is perceived as integral to their vision of meeting the needs of every child.

> There's always an adult in the classroom who will listen and talk to you. If I'm not happy then the task will be changed in some way so I understand how to improve and take things forward.
>
> (Ben)

Using TASC as a major strategy to address all pupils' needs has meant that the school has developed an assessment and monitoring profile that gives attention to qualitative learning processes and not just quantifiable outcomes. Staff feel that the TASC Process enables them to have the freedom to develop differentiated activities and to observe pupils closely whilst they are developing their negotiated independent activities. Questionnaires encourage and support peer self-evaluation and have been developed for both staff and pupils.

A 'traffic light system' devised against set criteria for projects is in operation and is fully understood by the pupils. Teachers encourage pupils to assess their own performance and to set personal targets. The pupils easily discuss how the shared roles within a TASC project offer them individual tasks that suit their strengths.

> TASC enables differentiation, it enables you to stretch from the baseline of where the child is. It allows the children the freedom to fly.
>
> (Year 2 class teacher)

> The TASC framework is applicable to all levels of ability, SEN pupils are supported and involved at one level and able pupils are stretched and challenged by delving deeper into a topic.
>
> (Class teacher)

> Individual needs are focused upon, challenge is provided and there is peer and self-assessment therefore giving cognisance to 'the rising tide lifts all ships'.
>
> (Deputy headteacher)

The TASC Strategy is used as a whole-class initiative and provides learners with a structure that can guide them through a totally personal learning experience. It is being used with all ages from Early Years to upper Key Stage 2, both for individual sessions and for longer term projects. During interviews with pupils it is clear that the pupils understand what the TASC Framework is and are able to show how the problem-solving process has supported them, first in setting their own agenda for learning and then pursuing it independently.

Monitoring and addressing the causes of underachievement

The staff strongly believe that, in order to redress *underdevelopment* of their pupils, they must focus on identifying and providing strategies to tackle underachievement wherever it may be found, be it a pupil with SEN or a pupil identified as potentially able.

Ollerton's main difficulties arise when social factors beyond their control impact on learning and cause underachievement. They address this by providing a safe, caring, supportive and enriched environment, by working within an ethos of learning together, with pupils learning from each other, and by setting high expectations for all within a culture where 'everyone can succeed'.

Work is planned to pupils' individual needs and pupils readily say that they find their learning interesting and enjoyable. Strategies for tackling underachievement, excellent support from a range of adults, all have a positive impact; and regular assessment of work allows teachers to set individual pupils targets for future learning.

Leadership

Although the remodelled school has been in existence for only two years, all staff have an enthusiasm, commitment and understanding to meeting the needs of able pupils. Staff feel that they are fully involved in planning: time has been taken to debate and discuss issues surrounding able pupils and identify areas for development particularly in addressing underachievement.

> We have been able to reflect on our practice, review and modify our provision as we have developed and gained in confidence.
>
> (Class teacher)

The headteacher is credited with setting high expectations and aspirations for all staff and pupils and is well informed about successes and areas for development. All staff have received specific G + T training on identification and how to set learning challenges. The drive for continuing improvement is supported by good self-evaluation processes which support the creation of the school improvement plan and inform future training needs.

The school has a specific school governor with designated responsibility for G + T. He ensures all governors are well informed about issues related to able pupils. Through meetings with the G + T coordinator and formal reports, the governor is able to talk about underachieving pupils and how the school develops strategies and monitors pupil progress. He is fully aware of the Individual Education Plans that are drawn up for underachievers and how they are closely monitored.

The following case study shows how Lanya, a young child of six years, can recognise and discuss her learning needs in the supportive, open atmosphere created by the school.

Case study of Lanya

Lanya is six years old and has no difficulty in identifying herself as an able pupil in her Year 2 class, but feels it is important that she isn't the only able pupil in her class:

> My friend, who is quieter than me, is just as good a reader and talker.

Lanya is a very happy, talkative child who is well motivated and loves coming to school. She paints a rich picture of her learning, both in and out of school. It is obvious she is linguistically very talented.

She discusses her favourite subjects and those that she feels she does well in. She loves the lessons where TASC is a feature. It is surprising for one so young that she can describe the TASC process, the elements of the process she enjoys and areas where she feels TASC restricts her. Lanya, at six years old, explains how pupils work in groups and what each child's role was in developing the Teddy Bears' Picnic.

She likes working in groups but feels that in a session where she has been the only girl, she has to lead to keep the boys on task; her final statement is:

> The boys are lazy; they like talking about their ideas but don't do the doing!

Lanya feels encouraged at school and is presented with work that

> makes me think . . . I like things that I can explore where there is no answer.

She talks about her reading and is able to recall, in detail, her favourite book and also how she thinks about a different ending to the story.

She explains how her teacher takes her to the town library to choose reading books and how this and the out-of-hours clubs have stopped her from becoming bored. Lanya appears to be very much aware and well informed of the enrichment and extension activities available; she also voices her opinion on what she thinks is missing.

Through TASC groups Lanya explains that she feels she can help pupils who are 'not as clever as myself'. She explains that she doesn't do the work for them but asks them questions:

> Sometimes I can see by their face they're puzzled so I explain; and if they are still not sure I think about another way I can show them. This helps me because I can go back to my work and make it better.

Lanya's discussions make it clear that TASC is a process that helps all levels of ability. Giving Lanya challenges is crucial if she is to continue to make progress and not become an underachiever.

> It's good when the work is hard, when it's easy I just do it straight away and then everything's boring.

Case study of Ben and Jordan

Ben and Jordan, at nine years old, explain clearly that each member of the group in their TASC-based 'Italy' project has very specific roles which suit the task; but Ben is able to show how he is pursuing an individual focus on Rome, which will extend the shared outcome. He is making a conscious choice about how to push his learning boundaries, challenging himself and creating a self-directed, personal learning experience. He brings additional resources and books from home. He is taking risks, but his peers support him, with the boys healthily competing with each other and providing appropriate challenge for all.

Case study 2: Hermitage Primary School

Contextual information

Hermitage School (www.hermitage.westberks.org) is a primary school situated near Newbury in rural West Berkshire where the social economic circumstances of pupils are very favourable. It is smaller than the average primary school with the number of pupils on role at 120 but was expected to expand to 180 in September 2007. The pupils come mainly from surrounding villages with 20 per cent of the pupils coming from the local army barracks. There is a small ethnic and cultural mix with negligible numbers of pupil on free school meals. Twenty per cent of the pupils are identified as SEN, many of whom fall in the Asperger's Autistic Spectrum; these pupils may also be identified as gifted or talented. Parents set high expectations for their children, but in doing so support the school in a variety of ways.

In October 2002, the Office for Standards in Education (Ofsted) labelled the school as an 'underachieving school' as a result of standards of attainment. Pupils entered the school with attainment above average and left with standards only average. The inspection report considered that more could be done to raise attainment at the top end of the ability range.

Over the past five years the situation has changed dramatically. Pupils at the end of Key Stage 1 now consistently achieve above national averages at Level 3 in English, and in mathematics they are in the top 5 per cent nationally. Pupils at the end Key Stage 2 at Level 5 perform well above the national average in English and mathematics. In science assessments outcomes put the school in the top 5 per cent nationally.

Using the NACE Challenge Award Framework

To redress the syndrome of general underachievement, the headteacher felt that all staff needed to work on a cohesive and effective strategy which would outline the best direction for identifying pupils and developing effective provision. The first step was to appoint a new senior teacher who had responsibility for developing provision for gifted and talented pupils. As the next step, through the support of the local authority, the school began to engage with the NACE Challenge Award Framework.

This process has provided all the staff in the school with a tool with which to audit existing provision, identify good practice and plan development, providing the vehicle to address the key issues raised by Ofsted. By following the Challenge Award Framework, the staff have ensured that their approach covers all aspects of quality provision and supports a whole school approach to raising standards.

The headteacher has now created an ethos where high expectations and high standards are expected and all learners are encouraged to strive for their best. Provision at Hermitage is now well embedded and when Ofsted visited they stated

> there has been good improvement since the last inspection, and the school is no longer judged to be underachieving. The overall achievement of high attaining pupils is now good across the school.

In order to create the appropriate opportunities and provision, the school acknowledges that it needs a clear rationale for identification that recognises all pupils' abilities and talents. The process includes sensitive observations by teachers and the negotiation of individual challenge plans with the pupils. Parents are also involved in this negotiation. Pupil tracking is now in place allowing the identification of underachievement at an early stage. The school strongly supports the philosophy of a personalised learning agenda and the ethos encourages every learner to 'be the best they can'.

The ethos in the school has changed: there has been a move away from playing safe, to creating a culture of exciting and innovative challenge for all pupils.

> It's better to challenge and support and rethink failure.
>
> (G +T coordinator)

Teachers challenge pupils to take risks and support them if things go wrong; this has helped the pupils to build self-confidence and self-belief and to motivate and engage them. Previously, acceleration was the only form of differentiation, and the school acknowledged this needed to change. Now, as a whole staff they look at different ways of differentiation which can be fed into pupils' individual challenge plans.

Learning is successfully extended through a wide variety of events, visits and out-of-hours activities. There is an extensive selection of activities ranging from art, sports and music, to literacy and numeracy enrichment clubs. The out-of-hours learning activities are available for all pupils, and it is important to note that those pupils who are on a targeted improvement programme may be encouraged to join a particular club to boost self-esteem, self-confidence and motivation.

There are special science, art and mathematics weeks, where experts come to the school to work with the school staff and pupils. A very successful mathematics project involved the pupils in running their own cake shop business in which they were engaged in the complete manufacturing process from making the packaging, designing and making the cakes, carrying out all the costing and finally working out the profit margin.

From Foundation Stage Profiles, the school is able to develop evidence that is carefully analysed in order to ensure that pupil progress is in line with potential. By engaging pupils in negotiating their own learning targets and monitoring their progress regularly, the value-added measure of relative progress made by pupils against the progress of pupils nationally and of pupils at similar schools is now well above average.

The headteacher, teachers, governors and parents have cooperated to build an inclusive school where all pupils are achieving well. The staff say:

> Working through the Challenge Award, which is no mean feat, cannot be accomplished without the support of the whole staff.
>
> (Deputy headteacher)

The school promotes the role of middle leaders and all subject coordinators are aware of their role in monitoring pupil progress. Planning is carefully scrutinised for challenge, and classroom observation monitors questioning and assessment. Verbal and written feedback is given to the gifted and talented coordinator who identifies areas of strength and good practice to share, and at the same time issues and areas are identified for development.

The following case study of Melanie reveals the confident awareness of a Year 6 child in discussing her learning needs.

Case study of Melanie

Melanie is 10.5 years old and is a confident mature able pupil in her school and is happy to talk about her experiences in Hermitage. She is well informed about what is happening in her school and explains that she has been identified as 'able' on entry to the school and has individual challenge plans. She explains how she negotiates challenging targets with the deputy head, Miss Carpenter:

> who you know is our G + T coordinator.

She explains that her targets are reviewed regularly and amended and that her mother comes into the school to review her targets:

> Miss talks to her about how she can support me at home. Sometimes I don't agree and we have a discussion and things are amended. I think it is very good that we are involved in planning our own learning; it motivates me and I think I set more challenging targets.

Melanie can talk about the wide range of enrichment and extension facilities that are on offer to her and feels privileged to be able to take advantage of the various events. She explains that she loves new challenges and experiences which motivate her to explore further.

Melanie feels she is very focused in school and is determined to do well. She likes lessons that allow her to think creatively, she enjoys group work and working in teams particularly where there is a competitive element. Her favourite subject is English and she spends time outside of school on her creative writing. Melanie clarifies that her choice of favourite subject changes depending on how confident she feels in the subject at the time.

> I used to have Maths as my favourite subject, I was top of the group, but I'm not as confident as I was. Maybe I need a TIP.

This statement confirms the positive way in which the pupils engage in their learning and are aware that there are structures in place to support them achieve.

Melanie values education, is clear about progression routes and talks about her future ambitions with clarity. She explains she is looking forward to going to secondary school and feels she has out grown primary school. She is obviously a very mature young lady who associates with older children rather than her peers.

When asked 'If you could change anything in lessons, what would it be?' She explains that she would love to be in a larger class with more than six girls in it. She realises that there advantages as well as disadvantages to a small school, but is excited about going to a large secondary school.

Melanie is proud to attend her school and feels the teachers work hard and plan interesting, active lessons that she finds challenging most of the time. She sees the school environment as safe, that the pupils have a say in their school, their opinions are listened to and she appreciates all the extra activities that the school offers.

Case study 3: Portswood Primary School

Contextual information

Portswood School (www.portswood.southampton.sch.uk) is a large primary school for pupils aged 4–11 years old. It serves a diverse population from across the City of Southampton with 70 per cent of the students coming from out of catchment areas. Pupils who attend the school come from widely varying communities ranging from areas with high levels of social deprivation to an affluent village. The population of over 400 pupils has a diverse cultural mix with over seventeen languages represented, with English a second or additional language for 42 per cent of the pupils. The school sees this culture diversity as enriching the lives of all its pupils.

In 1997, Ofsted recognised the school as being an underachieving, coasting school with provision for more able pupils being a key issue. Attainment of pupils at level 3 at the end of Key Stage 1 was in line with local and national averages. By the end of Key Stage 2 pupils' attainment at level 5 was also average.

In 2001, the school achieved Beacon status in recognition of its quality leadership and teaching. SATs results at the end of Key Stage 1 are now above average, with results at the end of Key Stage 2 improving year on year, moving from average to being amongst the top 5 per cent of all schools nationally.

Using the NACE Challenge Award Framework

What was the journey travelled? The school began a systematic review of its policy, practice and provision for all pupils. The focus was to create consistent pedagogy and practice across the whole school by transforming approaches to teaching and learning and developing opportunities to extend and enrich the curriculum, both in the classroom and through out-of-hours learning.

The NACE Challenge Award was used as the Framework to develop, monitor and evaluate provision for gifted and talented pupils. The Framework enabled staff to understand where they were going strategically and consolidated the vision for the whole school in meeting the needs of able pupils. The Framework was used as an effective self- review tool which supported clear progression and action planning for the future. (See Appendices 2 and 3.)

Portswood provision for gifted and talented pupils is an excellent example of how developing an ethos of challenging, extending and enriching all pupils' thinking, understanding, knowledge and skills impacts on attainment of all groups.

> Our provision is not about able children it's for all children . . . setting high expectations and high aspirations.
>
> (Able child coordinator)

> Enrichment and extension activities are in the classroom all the time, integral to all that is done . . . provision is not about bolt-on extras.'
>
> (Professional tutor)

> It is the approach to teaching and learning within the curriculum that is consistently applied across the school that is making the greatest impact on raising achievement.
>
> (Able pupil coordinator)

The set of core principles at the heart of improving provision are consistently applied by all staff. In Portswood you would see:

- an enriched and relevant curriculum delivered in a creative and stimulating learning environment;
- class work that is appropriately differentiated so that the curriculum provision adequately challenges the needs of and extends able and talented children through extension and enrichment, including homework;
- independent, open-ended tasks;
- the provision of additional opportunities which are open to all pupils but accommodates the special interests of individuals;
- children experiencing success in order to gain self-confidence and also being encouraged to take risks and make mistakes;
- able and talented children given extensive control over the direction of their learning;
- excellent access to ICT resources including the use of CD-ROMs and the Internet;
- pupils given opportunities to work with older children;
- extra-curricular clubs such as the school newspaper, *Planet Portswood*;
- musical and sporting opportunities;
- positive encouragement of parents and outside agencies.

For a school with such a diverse intake and a high percentage of children for whom English is an additional language, progress made is well above average. Attainment levels for pupils identified as gifted and talented have been steadily rising. Value-added data also indicates that Portswood achieves exceptionally well, especially for high attainers.

> Pride, passion and success is the experience we hope for every learner in Portswood.
>
> (Headteacher)

> The learning logs have the potential to improve provision and contribute to the growing agenda related to teaching out most able pupils.
>
> (Able pupil coordinator)

> Children skip towards their lessons; they're engaged and excited by exploring their own learning.
>
> (Class teacher)

> The leadership in the school is inspirational, setting high expectations and aspirations for all within a secure, safe and supportive environment.
>
> (Governor)

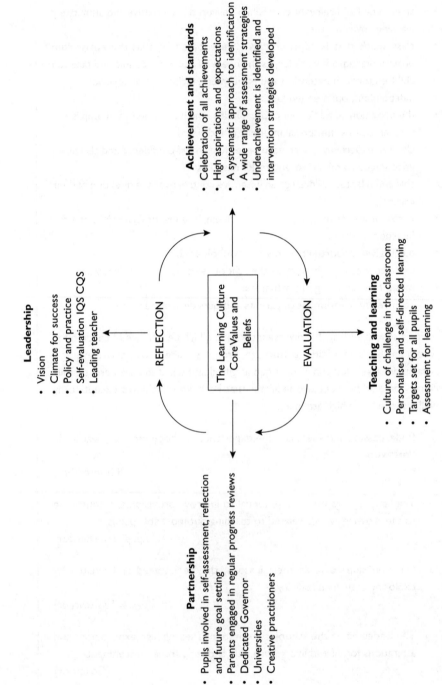

Leadership
- Vision
- Climate for success
- Policy and practice
- Self-evaluation IQS CQS
- Leading teacher

Achievement and standards
- Celebration of all achievements
- High aspirations and expectations
- A systematic approach to identification
- A wide range of assessment strategies
- Underachievement is identified and intervention strategies developed

REFLECTION

The Learning Culture Core Values and Beliefs

EVALUATION

Partnership
- Pupils involved in self-assessment, reflection and future goal setting
- Parents engaged in regular progress reviews
- Dedicated Governor
- Universities
- Creative practitioners

Teaching and learning
- Culture of challenge in the classroom
- Personalised and self-directed learning
- Targets set for all pupils
- Assessment for learning

Figure 6.1 Summary concept map 6

References and further reading

Bowden, B. (2003) *The Bowden Way – 50 Years of Leadership Wisdom*. Atlanta, GA: Longstreet Press Incorporated.

George, D. (2003) *Gifted Education: Identification and Provision*. London: Taylor & Francis.

Gilbert, C. (2006) *2020 Vision*. DfES, 04255–2006.

Renzulli, J. (1977) *The Schoolwide Enrichment Model* (SEM). Mansfield Center, CT: Creative Learning Press.

Wallace, B., Fitton, S., Leyden, S., Montgomery, D., Pomerantz, M. and Winstanley, C. (2007) *Raising the Achievement of Able, Gifted and Talented Pupils within an Inclusive School Framework: Guidelines for Schools to Audit and Extend Existing Best Practice*. Oxford: National Association for Able Children in Education. publications@nace.co.uk.

Conclusion and personal reflection

Belle Wallace

If readers will allow me to present a very personal conclusion, I would like to invite you to reflect on why we entered the teaching profession when we were deciding on a career path. Most of us were very young in years and experience, but I am sure that we were fired with enthusiasm for teaching and inspiring children and young people to be excited by their learning. As we all know to our personal cost, various pressures imposed by seemingly endless government initiatives and the increasing social and economic complexities of everyday living have often degraded our enthusiasm almost to exhaustion, and we get to the end of a school term grateful to have just survived! Only dedicated teachers know the deep tiredness of having worked with groups of children and young people in socially, emotionally and physically demanding classrooms.

But let us remind ourselves of why we entered the teaching profession in the first place. Didn't we want to practise the following ideals?

- The development of learners' ownership of their learning through the negotiation of relevant problems to be solved in relation to real-life learning and understanding;
- The development of constructive dialogue and interaction in the learning/teaching dynamic with reciprocity and equality of teachers and learners as jointly negotiating and constructing meaning;
- The development of learners' self-confidence and independence in decision-making and actions leading to their self-actualisation;
- The mutual respect derived from active listening and talking.

(Freire, 1998a, 1998b)

Yet most of our personal learning experiences had fallen very neatly into Freire's 'banking' concept of education. Information was dispensed to us to learn in order to fill up our 'empty' minds, and we dutifully memorised and regurgitated it for tests and examinations. So how did we develop the understanding of what I would call 'enabling and empowering learning and teaching processes'? I suggest that collectively we developed these ideals because good teachers are intuitively aware of how learners can best learn and, consequently, how we can best teach. Good teachers are socially and emotionally 'gifted' in the real sense that they *do* understand the needs of learners and, if given the creative freedom to develop their professional expertise, they become experts within their profession.

We intuitively know that:

- when learners' motivation is high, they are confident to take risks with expressing creative ideas, however tentative that expression may be;
- when learners have high self-confidence and good self-image, they are more open to accepting adaptations to their everyday life-styles, taking on new roles with high expectations of themselves;
- low levels of personal and classroom anxieties are indispensable for learners to make progress.

(Dromi, 1993, Krashen, 1981)

We also know that:

- learners develop language and cognitive skills through purposeful real-life situations that provide them with authentic and meaningful contexts for learning;
- learning to think and talk effectively are active processes – it is not possible to 'do language and thinking to learners', they must do it for themselves;
- it is not sufficient for learners to learn knowledge, they need to do something constructive with the knowledge;
- both language and thinking skills are vehicles for self-expression, personalisation and ownership of the learning processes;
- the development of language and thinking skills must be active processes and transferred across the curriculum;
- teachers and learners need to negotiate curriculum topics, developing these topics together with a range of appropriate teaching/learning processes that develop learners' positive self-image, internal locus of control and the belief in lifelong learning.

(Wallace, 1993)

In the past twenty years, we have witnessed the increasing mechanisation of the teaching and learning processes in schools and in other areas of public life brought about by the insistence of the government on 'measurable' achievement targets and 'universal' standards. Teachers are certainly not against the need for learners and teachers striving to reach goals; but not every learning goal can be quantified and measured, organised statistically and then compared and contrasted in what came to be labelled 'the shame and blame culture'. Teachers have reported that they have been treated as mechanical technicians delivering set content, rather than as educators interacting with learners. They have reported that increasing numbers of pupils have consequently become de-motivated and anti-school.

However, the climate in education has modified and become far more liberal in recent years: the new Strategy Documents encourage greater flexibility of approaches, invite teachers to work creatively and emphasise the importance of problem-solving and thinking skills. The current 'buzz' words are 'personalised and independent learning', 'learner decision-making and ownership', 'children as researchers', 'out-of-hours and off-site learning'. Schools are rejoicing in the freedom this gives to develop new modes of classroom interaction and school organisation. The case studies of schools, undoubtedly, are typical of many similarly good schools. It has been a joy and a privilege, however, to have been made so welcome in the twelve particular schools that have been so honest in the sharing and appraisal of their practices. It is also a privilege to be able to share and reflect on strategies for best practice with you, the reader, who will, undoubtedly, identify with the ideas shared within this text.

The authors of this text hope they have renewed your ideals in education and given you the courage to trust your own intuitive judgements about the best practices that underpin learning and teaching.

References and further reading

Dromi, E. (1993) 'Language and cognition: a developmental perspective', in Dromi, E. (ed.) *Language and Cognition: A Developmental Perspective*. Volume 5. Norwood, NJ: Ablex.

Freire, P. (1998a) *Pedagogy of Hope*. New York: Continuum.

Freire, P. (1998b) *Pedagogy of the Oppressed*. New revised 20th anniversary edn. New York: Continuum.

Krashen, S. D. (1981) *Second Language Acquisition and Second Language Learning*. New York: Pergamon Press.

Wallace, B. and Maker, C. J. *et al.* (2004) *Teaching Problem-Solving and Thinking Skills: An Inclusive Approach*. London: David Fulton Publishers.

Appendix 1

Contextual data of the participating case-study schools

Burlington Junior School, New Malden, Surrey KT3 4LT

Burlington School (www.burlingtonjunior.co.uk) is a non-denominational mixed community school for 7–11 year olds with around 360–380 pupils on roll. The pupils represent a wide range of social backgrounds and there are almost 60 per cent of pupils with English as an Additional Language (EAL). Twenty-one different languages are spoken, mainly English, Tamil, Urdu, Gujerati and Korean. Around 20 per cent enter the school later than the usual time of entry and many of these pupils speak very little English. An average number of pupils have special educational needs and slightly less than average require school meals.

Farnborough Primary School, London Borough of Bromley

Farnborough (www.farnborough.bromley.sch.uk) is a mixed one-form entry community school with phased entry into the Reception year. At present there are around 220 pupils in the school and eight members of full-time staff in addition to the headteacher. The size of the school is typical of most primary schools nationally. The number of pupils on the special needs register is above the national average at 25.4 per cent and the percentage of pupils with statements is 1.8 per cent. The pupils' special needs are mainly in the area of SEBD and speech and communication difficulties. There are 3.8 per cent of pupils with English as a second language and 10.7 per cent of the pupils come from minority ethnic backgrounds. On entry to the school the pupils' attainment is wide ranging but broadly average overall. They come from homes that are socio-economically diverse and 4.1 per cent are eligible for free school meals. Not all the children joining the school have experienced the Foundation Stage Programme or have been assessed against the Foundation Stage Profile.

Grafton Primary School, London Borough of Holloway

Grafton (www.graftonschool.co.uk) is an inner-city primary school for some 450 children from 3 years 6 months to 11 years old. The school is a very diverse community with a rich ethnic mix. The school serves an area whose socio-economic circumstances are much lower than usually found. More than 50 per cent of the pupils are entitled to free school meals and a similar proportion have learning and emotional difficulties with a high number of children experiencing Language and Communication needs. Slightly more than 50 per cent of the pupils are from ethnic minority backgrounds; the largest groups being Black African and Caribbean. There are 60 per cent of the pupils with a first language that is not English, but is predominantly Turkish, Somali, Bengali, Spanish and Italian. All school signs are in the three main languages of the school, English, Turkish and Bengali and translators and translations are widely available including Spanish and Italian.

Hermitage Primary School, West Berks

Hermitage School (www.hermitage.westberks.org) is a smaller than the average, but expanding, rural primary school in Newbury, West Berkshire. There is a small ethnic and cultural mix with negligible numbers of pupils on free school meals. There are 20 per cent of pupils identified as SEN, many of whom fall in the Asperger's Autistic Spectrum; some of these pupils may also be identified as Gifted or Talented. Parents set high expectations for their children, but in doing so support the school in a variety of ways. Ofsted (2002) labelled the school as an 'underachieving school' as a result of standards of attainment. Pupils entered the school with attainment above average and left with standards only average. The inspection report considered that more could be done to raise attainment at the top end of the ability range.

Lowes Wong Junior School, Southwell, Nottinghamshire

Lowes Wong Anglican Methodist School (www.loweswong-jun.notts.sch.uk) is a large junior school in the small market town of Southwell. It serves a mixed, but relatively prosperous catchment area and has currently 398 pupils on roll in the school. There are only a few pupils from ethnic minority backgrounds, but it is an inclusive school. Lowes Wong Junior is a high achieving school with a long-standing reputation for high expectations and achievements. Although the percentage of children with special needs is low, the school has been very successful in meeting the needs of children who struggle with their learning or behaviour. The provision for the most able and talented pupils took a step forward with the appointment, five years ago, of the present headteacher, who has been involved in curriculum development and training in able children's education for a number of years. The school is currently a model of exciting and innovative practice, where music, dance, drama and sport are major strengths.

Ollerton Primary School, Nottinghamshire

Ollerton Primary School (www.ollertonprimary.notts.sch.uk) has 300 pupils from Foundation to Year 6. Recently reorganised, it serves the ex-mining communities of Ollerton, New Ollerton and Boughton, which are within one of the most disadvantaged wards within Nottinghamshire. There is high unemployment and high levels of social deprivation: nearly 50 per cent of the pupils are known to be eligible for free school meals and the number of pupils who are on the special needs register is well above the national average. There is high pupil mobility with a growing number of pupils who have joined, then left and later rejoined the school. There is also a significant number of Looked After children with complex needs. There is a minority ethnic and cultural mix; and no pupils with English as a second language. The attainment of pupils on entry to full-time schooling is well below the local authority average for both literacy and numeracy. All pupils make good progress and the standards achieved by pupils are high in relation to similar schools and are improving steadily when compared to all schools.

Portswood Primary School, Southampton

Portswood School (www.portswood.southampton.sch.uk) is a mixed primary school of 400 pupils, serving a diverse population from across the City of Southampton with 70 per cent of the students coming from out of catchment area. Pupils come from widely varying communities ranging from areas with high levels of social deprivation to a range of affluent villages. The school population has a diverse cultural mix with over seventeen languages represented, with English, a second or additional language for 42 per cent of the pupils. The school sees this culture diversity as enriching the lives of all its pupils whose attainment on entry to the Reception is above the national and local averages. Those pupils identified as having special educational needs is below the national average. There are 36 per cent of pupils on the able register with English as an additional language.

Homewood and Sixth Form Centre Arts College, Tenterden, Kent

Homewood School (www.homewood-school.co.uk) is a non-denominational mixed Foundation school for 11–18 year olds with Specialist status in Performing Arts and Art. It has 2082 pupils on roll and falls within the

Comprehensive System in Kent. Homewood School applies its own entry criteria: all pupils applying to the school are assessed and 20 per cent are admitted 'with reference to their aptitude and ability'. The remaining 80 per cent of pupils are admitted 'without reference to their aptitude and ability'. The one exception to this is that each year, four pupils are admitted to Year 7 on the basis of exceptional musical ability which is usually measured as standard Grade 4 or above (instrumental/voice). There are less than average pupils with special educational needs, but there is a broad social demographic since the school sits within a comprehensive system inside a selective county.

Lampton School, London Borough of Hounslow

Lampton School (www.lampton.hounslow.sch.uk) provides a mixed, comprehensive education to a truly multicultural population of 1382 pupils ranging in age from 11 to 18. This figure includes 315 pupils in the Sixth Form. It is a now a very popular school and is oversubscribed with at least 150 applicants who have not secured places for September 2007 and who may appeal, seeking a place at this community school. Ten years ago it only attracted about 107 applications for 210 places in Year 7. The majority of the pupils come from four world religions: Christianity, Hinduism, Islam and Sikhism. The school takes take pride in their reputation for mutual respect and tolerance for all. Their last Ofsted report (and many visitors) commented on the positive relationships throughout the school. Other key indicators describing the school are as follows: 21 per cent Free School Meals; 3.2 per cent Statemented; 14.5 per cent School Action (SEN); 3.2 per cent School Action Plus; 78.1 per cent Minority Ethnic Pupils; 66.8 per cent EAL (English as an Additional Language) stages 1–4.

Newstead Wood School for Girls, London Borough of Bromley

Newstead Wood School for Girls (www.newsteadwood.bromley.sch.uk/) is a Foundation, Selective, 11–18 Engineering Specialist School with a particular focus on the application of science, mathematics and technology. It is located in Orpington within the London Borough of Bromley. Admissions are based upon an application to the school and the local authority, a residence within a given radius of the school, and both verbal and non-verbal reasoning tests which take place annually in November. Successful applicants have scores within the top 130 places and about 750 pupils apply each year. Newstead Wood draws pupils from over sixty primary schools. There are over 950 pupils in this educational setting.

Seven Kings High School in the London Borough of Redbridge, Ilford

Seven Kings High School (public.skhs.net) is a specialist school for Science, Technology, Modern Foreign Languages; designated a Beacon and Leading Edge School; the local authority school for pupils with physical disability; a Training School; several times winner of the government's Excellent Achievement Award; six form entry (11 to 18), co-educational, comprehensive, mixed ability, multi-ethnic, multilingual (70–80 languages spoken).

The school motto is Friendship, Excellence and Opportunity. Staff are particularly proud of their involvement on the 'Learn How to Learn' project with a key focus on 'Assessment for Learning' – a national action research project on assessment and learning.

St Marylebone School, London Borough of Westminster

St Marylebone School (http://intranet.stmarylebone.westminster.sch.uk/) is an 11–18 comprehensive Church of England school for girls, with mixed entry post-16. The school draws from 30+ primary schools and has a population of around 850 students. It represents a diverse ethnic and cultural mix, including a high percentage of students from European countries. Over thirty languages are represented in the school. English is a second or additional language for more than 50 per cent of the students. The Central London Learning Skills Council identifies the school's catchment area as one of the most deprived nationally. Around 40 per cent of students are entitled to free school meals. In 1998 the school achieved specialist school status for the Performing Arts. In 2006 it achieved an additional specialism for Maths and Computing. It has also been awarded the Gold Artmark. Value-added data also indicate that St Marylebone School achieves exceptionally well, especially for able students.

Appendix 2

Able, gifted and talented child referral sheet (Portswood)

Name _____ Class 4S _____ Teacher making referral _____

Able, Gifted or Talented (and learning area)	What sources of evidence do you have for this referral?	School criteria
Able – English Speaking and Listening Reading Writing Science History Geography ICT PE	Top Group – English, Maths, Science Excellent public speaking; drama assemblies – leading role Yr3 Level 4c reading Yr3 Level 3a writing Yr3 Level 3b maths Yr3 Level 4a science Written and oral responses in WWII/Ancient Greece (History) Droxford (Geography)	• Able children – a group of children (20 per cent of our school population) that show high levels of attainment in their general intellectual ability, specific academic ability, creative thinking, technical ability and/or interpersonal skills. This group includes subgroups of more-able and gifted.

Extension activities required for ICT – Top Group member

Excellent gymnastic performance – communication of ideas clear – demonstrates to class

Reading age – Jun 05 = 12 yr+

Spelling age – Jun 05 = 13.4 yr

- Gifted – a minority of children (0.5 per cent or less of our school population) who are capable of exceptional in one or more areas of the curriculum and are working one key stage above their peers.
- Talented – a group of children (20 per cent of our school population) who excel at sports, games or the visual and performing arts.

Appendix 3

Flexible long-term planning for able learner profiled in Appendix 2

Subject	General provision	Autumn	Spring	Summer
Literacy	Speaking + Listening Present work in plenary. Key part in public speaking. Opportunities for role plays/debates.	Speaking + Listening Key part in Y4 Harvest assembly. Give the opportunity in script writing to perform as extension to activity. Key part in Christmas performance.	Speaking + Listening Key part in Y4 assembly. Opportunity to present report on Wasteland, pairing able S+L children together. Key role in Romans invading Britain debate.	Speaking + Listening Key speaking/lead role in end of year performance. Key part in class assembly. Drama in literacy – trip to the zoo. Focus on responding to others.
	Writing Teach objectives for year above.	Writing Work with J as a response partner to evaluate their own and others'	Writing Work with J as a response partner to evaluate their own	Writing Work with R as a response partner to

evaluate their own and others' work before and after completion.
Introduce to abbreviated 'ispace' – 'SAC' to encourage progression in their writing.
Include a success criteria of own choosing when writing.
Extended writing – write story in an able children pair in same class.
Use of laptops during poetry lessons to produce work.
In pairs, produce recording of a guided tour of school (rest of class doing it in groups of 4).
Independent research (Internet/books) into different types of poems, cinquains, haikus etc. and share findings/preferences with class.

and others' work before and after completion.
Focus – writing, both narrative and non-fiction forms, towards a defined conclusion.
Use of laptops during lessons to produce work.
Descriptive writing and expressive vocabulary in poetry form – children to read, respond to and write in the style of a range of genres.
Extended writing – write 'Borrowers' story in an able children pair in same class.

Additional use of ICT.

work before completion.

Subject	General provision	Autumn	Spring	Summer
	Reading Focus on Level 4 reading objectives – Provide opportunity to read in whole class situations. Focus teaching in guided reading on specific skills. Meet AG&T manager for reading conference half termly.	Reading Complete reading log entries for all – some. Read once a week with partner from Y3 – a couple of sessions completed. Focus – recognise how characters are presented in different ways and respond to this with reference to the text.	Reading Complete reading log entries for all books read at home and at school – majority of books read were logged. Read once a week with partner from Y4, with KW supervising, focusing on *The Snow Spider*.	Reading Complete detailed reading log entries for all books read, at home and at school. Pre-prep and read some of class story – *The Silver Sword*.
Science	Encourage independence when designing investigations. Ensure greater precision and accuracy. Encourage higher-order thinking/explanations of findings.	Extend knowledge of circuits, view in detail the effects of series and parallel circuits and where they would be used. Research into different types of electricity and compare. AGT to work together to design experiment to investigate friction/ air resistance.	Encourage early on to think about the changing processes of solids and liquids and present ideas to class. Able children as a group to design own experiment to compare to class's experiment (water volume – conservation, melting solids – liquids, separating solids). Allow them to carry out own experiments if ideas different from class experiments. Expect detailed explanations of the changing processes of solids and liquids and encourage use of Internet and books to help with this.	Mixed ability pairings when researching muscles and developing working models – support the LA and revise own knowledge of muscle structure. Include opportunities for HA to take responsibility for learning. Selection of resources where the research skills and time allocation are left up to the individual. Independent preparation for future lesson – photograph different habitats with LSA support. Create own classifications key for made up animals.

History	Compare evidence/facts learnt across periods of history learnt. Role play.	N/A	Link learning of Romans back to Ancient Greece work from Y3. Encourage use of non-fiction books and Internet to conduct research to provide feedback to class – set as homework. Research Butser Hill prior to visit to brief class on what they will see.	In HA groups, plan own investigation into which environments woodlice prefer.
Geography	Provide opportunity for presentation/explanation to class. Create resources for lessons. Give opportunities to carry out independent research to enrich area of geographical investigation – St Mary's.	Extend study of local area to include improvements that could be made for specific groups of people including religions, handicap accessibility. How could we make Portswood a more health conscious environment? Work with Y3 AGT on writing directions from Portswood to Droxford. Use OS four-figure grid references accurately.	N/A	Encourage individual research early on in topic to inform the rest of the class of parts of a river and the water cycle. Allow the opportunity for the area experts (different sections of a river to be explored in detail and presented to the class).

N/A

Subject	General provision	Autumn	Spring	Summer
ICT	Independent use of laptops across the curriculum subjects. Independent selection of appropriate programmes/packages. Allow opportunities to experiment with other programmes.	Use of shortcut keys: Ctrl C, Ctrl V, Ctrl X. Encourage completion of newspaper to printed standard. The paper to include: topic-related sections, articles by other authors, advertisements, offers.	During Superlogo work, provide opportunities to explore forming instructions and procedures before guidance is given. Expect formulae and procedures to be found for complicated shapes and patterns. Encourage use of shortcuts for instructions e.g. Lt 90, 10 (Rt 180, Lt 65). Encourage sessions where children are requested to support lower ability allowing them to explain their skills to others.	Create larger databases with greater number of fields. Higher expectations in level of fluidity within a database – are all the fields clear, relevant and in sensible order? Greater responsibility in organising and running logistics of obtaining data from various year groups in the school.
PE	Encourage attendance at after-school sports clubs. Show skills to others, with commentary. Develop vocabulary.	Allow time to prepare and lead warm-up activities and show skills in: travelling unit, e.g. stretching, forward rolls, backward rolls, cartwheels. Chinese dance e.g. push/pull movements.	Allow time to prepare and lead warm-up activities and show skills in: jumping unit e.g. stretching, jumping sequences, group work. Use of higher vaults.	Allow time to prepare and lead warm-up of activity and show skills in: balancing/rolling unit e.g. stretching, balancing sequences, group work, correct forward roll.

Index